PYTHON DATA SCIENCE

Data is the new oil. Data processing, analysis and visualization are must have skills for Data Scientists. This book is created for those who are about to step in the path to become data scientists.
And we will do that using Python, not only the most popular but also, the best choice to work with data. This book is meant for the people familiar with Python as,
this book will not focus on the Python basics. We will work using libraries and packages like Numpy, SciPy, Pandas, Matplotlib, etc.

A complete guidebook for anyone who wants to master data analysis, processing and visualization using Python.

Rahul Mula

Data Science with Python
by Rahul Mula
© 2020 Data Science with Python
All rights reserved. No portion of this book may be reproduced in any form without permission from the copyright holder, except as permitted by U.S. copyright law.
Cover by Rahul Mula.
All the programs written in this book are tested and verified by the author.
Template from freepik.com

ISBN : 979-8-69-981909-6

Preface

Why should you learn data science? or what are its uses? Would be the questions that may come to your mind. The answer is simple, think that you are given a data from a shop, about its sales. The data has a product name, its quantity, rate, amount, and time purchased columns with several hundred rows of products. If you want to perform some analysis like the product which is most purchased in that day, it will take a lot of time to do it manually. To ease up these tasks, we use data analysis, i.e. we run a program with codes to perform a certain data analysis. The computer runs the program and we get the output in just few seconds.

So, How to do that? Well, we need to learn Data Science to perform tasks like data analysis, processing and visualization.

This book is prepared especially for beginners (at Data Science), but you should be familiar with programming in Python. We will work with packages and modules like NumPy, SciPy, Pandas and Matplotlib to perform analysis and other tasks. I kept this book open to the basic concepts to help beginners to understand everything and also included advanced topics to not limit you to the basics. Data science may seem tough and boring, but as you handle more and more data, you'll play with it! So, I wish you best luck to your journey to become a Data Scientist.

CONTENTS

01 CHAPTER

DATA SCIENCE INTRODUCTION
- What is Data Science?
- How to work with data?
- Why use Python?

02 CHAPTER

SETTING-UP ENVIRONMENT
- Installing Anaconda
- Jupyter Notebook
- Working with Jupyter Notebook

03 CHAPTER

PANDAS LIBRARY
- Features of Pandas Library
- Series
- Data Frames

04 CHAPTER

NUMPY PACKAGE
- Features of NumPy
- ndarray Objects
- List vs. ndarrays

05 CHAPTER

SCIPY PACKAGE
- Features of SciPy
- Data Structures
- SciPy Sub-Packages

06 CHAPTER
MATPLOTLIB LIBRARY
- Features of Matplotlib
- Data Visualization
- PyPlot in Matplotlib

CONTENTS

07 CHAPTER

DATA OPERATIONS AND CLEANSING
- Numpy Operations
- Pandas Operations
- Slicing Syntax

08 CHAPTER

DATA PROCESSING
- Processing CSV Data
- Processing JSON Data
- Processing XLS Data

09 CHAPTER

PYTHON DATABASES
- Databases
- Relational Databases

10 CHAPTER

DATA WRANGLING AND AGGREGATION
- Concatenating Data
- Grouping Data
- Applying aggregates on DataFrame

11 CHAPTER

READING HTML PAGES
- Beautiful Soap Package
- Reading HTML content
- Working with tag values

12 CHAPTER

DATA SPECIFICATION
- Working with unstructured data
- Word Tokenization
- Stemming and Lemmatization

CONTENTS

CHAPTER 13

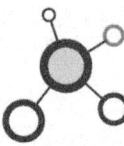

DATA VISUALIZATION
- Pandas, Numpy & Matplotlib
- Plotting a Chart
- Editing labels and colors
- Adding Annotations
- Adding Legends
- Box Plots
- Plotting Heat Maps
- Scatter Plots
- Plotting Bubble Charts
- Plotting 3D Charts
- Time Series
- Plotting graphs
- Sparse graphs

CHAPTER 14

MEASURING DATA
- Calculating Mean and Median
- Calculating Mode
- Measuring Variance

CHAPTER 15

DATA DISTRIBUTION
- Normal & Binomial Distribution
- Poisson Distribution
- Bernoulli Distribution

CHAPTER 16

DATA TESTS
- P-Value
- Correlations
- Chi-Square Test

CHAPTER 17

PROJECT
- Test Your Knowledge

01 DATA SCIENCE INTRODUCTION

- What is Data Science?
- How to work with data?
- Why use Python?

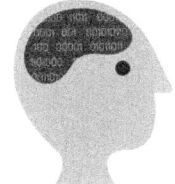

01 DATA SCIENCE INTRODUCTION

What is Data Science?

"
**Data is what you need to do ANALYTICS,
Information is what you need to do BUSSINESS.**

Commonly referred to as the *"Oil of the 21st century"* our digital data carries the most importance in the field. It has incalculable benefits in business, research and our everyday lives.

Your route to work, your most recent Google search for the nearest coffee shop, your Instagram post about what you ate, and even the health data from your fitness tracker are all the important to different data scientists in different ways. Sifting through massive lakes of data, looking for connections and patterns, data science is responsible for bringing us new products, delivering breakthrough insights and making our lives more convenient.

03 DATA SCIENCE INTRODUCTION

How to work with Data?

Data science involves a plethora of disciplines and expertise areas to produce a holistic, thorough and refined look into raw data. Data scientists must be skilled in everything from data engineering, math, statistics, advanced computing and visualizations to be able to effectively sift through muddled masses of information and communicate only the most vital bits that will help drive innovation and efficiency.

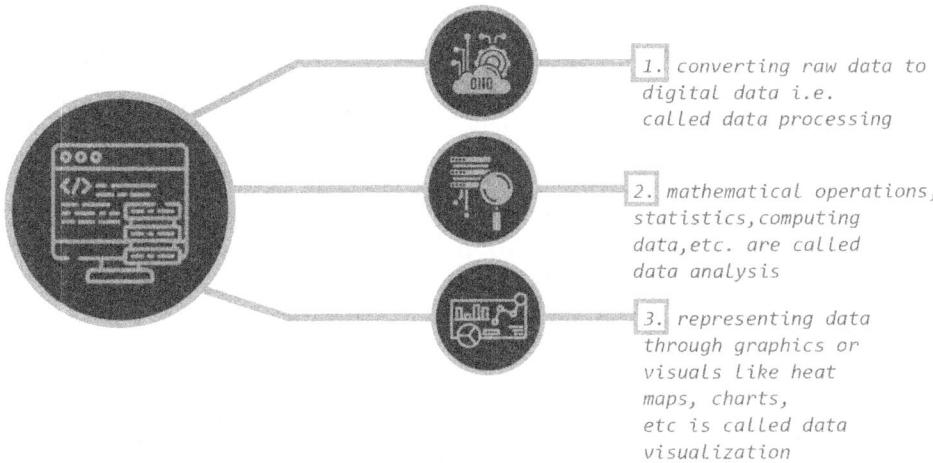

1. converting raw data to digital data i.e. called data processing

2. mathematical operations, statistics, computing data, etc. are called data analysis

3. representing data through graphics or visuals like heat maps, charts, etc is called data visualization

We will cover each step of data processing, analysing and visualizing in sub-steps to the get the grasp of everything individually.

Except for the above procedures, artificial intelligence also plays a major role i.e. computing. We may have the knowledge how to process, analyize or visualize data but, if we do all those manually it will take weeks or even months, some large amount of data are not even possible to be analysed by people alone. To share the workload and accelarate the procedure, we rely upon computers, which processes large amount data in mere seconds or milli-seconds. So, without manpower computers are worth nothing and without computers people are hopeless.

04 | DATA SCIENCE INTRODUCTION

Why Choose Python?

The programming requirements of data science demands a very versatile yet flexible language which is simple to code but can handle highly complex mathematical processing. Python is most suited for such requirements as it has already established itself both as a language for general computing as well as scientific computing. More over it is being continuously upgraded in form of new addition to its vast amount of libraries aimed at different programming requirements. Python has all the features needed for our requirements like:

- Python is the most beginner freindly language, which easy to learn.
- Python is also a dynamically-typed language, i.e. Python codes are lesser than other programming languages like, R.
- It is cross platform, so the same code works in multiple environments without needing any change.
- It executes faster than other similar languages used for data analysis like R and MATLAB.
- Its excellent memory management capability, especially garbage collection makes it versatile in gracefully managing very large volume of data transformation, slicing, dicing and visualization.
- Most importantly Python has got a very large collection of libraries which serve as special purpose analysis tools like, NumPy, Scipy, etc.
- Python has packages which can directly use the code from other languages like Java or C. This helps in optimizing the code performance by using existing code of other languages, whenever it gives a better result.

02 SETTING-UP ENVIRONMENT

- Installing Anaconda
- Jupyter notebook
- Working with Jupyter notebook

# 02 SETTING-UP ENVIRONMENT

Installing Anaconda

Head to anaconda.com/products/individual to download the latest version of Anaconda.

You can download the anaconda-installer for your system, whether it is Windows, Mac or Linux. After installing it, just run the installer and install it as usual.

After installation, search for anaconda prompt and run it.

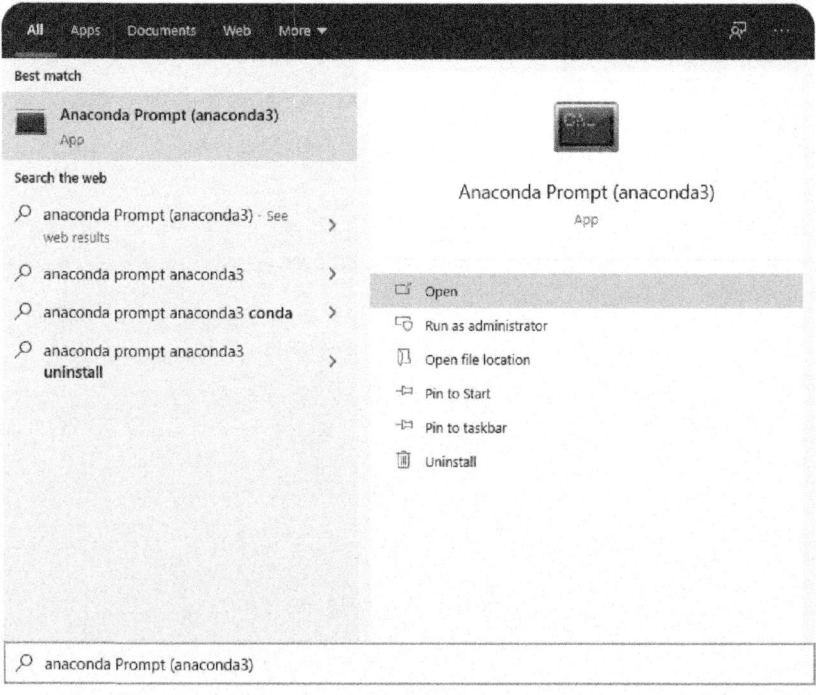

07 SETTING-UP ENVIRONMENT

This is the Anaconda Command Prompt, from where we can run programs or perform other operations using code's as commands.

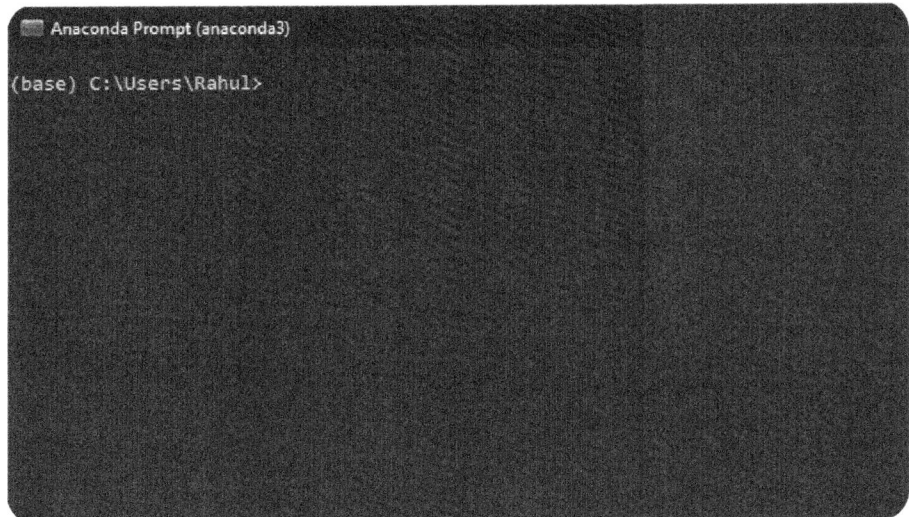

Jupyter Notebook

The Jupyter Notebook is an open-source web application that allows you to create and share documents that contain live code, equations, visualizations and explanatory text. We will use it to perform our data processing, analytics and visualization on the go.

To open Jupter Notebook, write jupyter notebook in the anaconda command prompt and press enter.

08 SETTING-UP ENVIRONMENT

![Anaconda Prompt jupyter notebook screenshot]

Anaconda will redirect you to your browser, [it may ask you, in which browser to host your jupyter notebook if you have more than one browsers] a new tab will appear with your Jupyter notebook hosted. You can host your Python files here, and also run the code on the fly.

In Jupyter Notebook, we don't need to install any other module, package or library externally everything we need is already present here and the best thing is that you can code online without installing any IDE or the Python Interpreter, which makes it the best choice for data scientists.

Working with Jupyter Notebook

To start coding, click on **New** and select **Python 3** to open a new Python file.

This is the place where we will write our code [in the cell] and run it.

If you cannot create new file or encounter any error, you can head directly to jupyter.org/try and choose Python.

10 SETTING-UP ENVIRONMENT

We can rename our file, by clicking the name
[untitled]

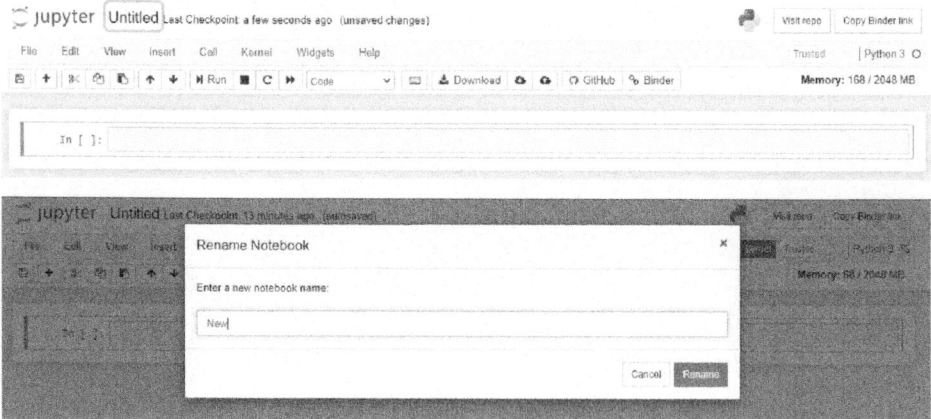

We have only one code cell, in this cell we will
write our code

There are three type cells - code cells, markdown
cells and raw cells.
We can use markdown cells to display headings or
titles.

Now run the cell by clicking the run button on the
header.

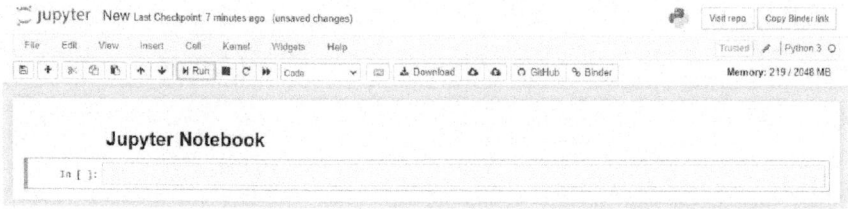

11 SETTING-UP ENVIRONMENT

In code cells, we can write Python codes and execute them instantly.

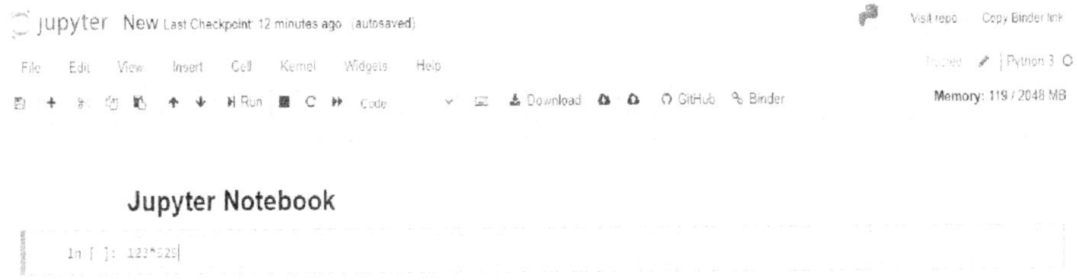

To insert a new cell below the selected cell, press **b** on your keyborad or click the **+** icon.

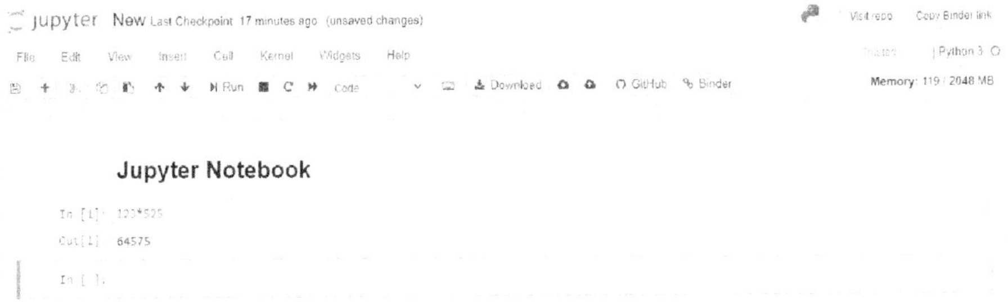

You can select [blue] or edit [green] a cell, by clicking outside the text feild or inside the text feild respectively.

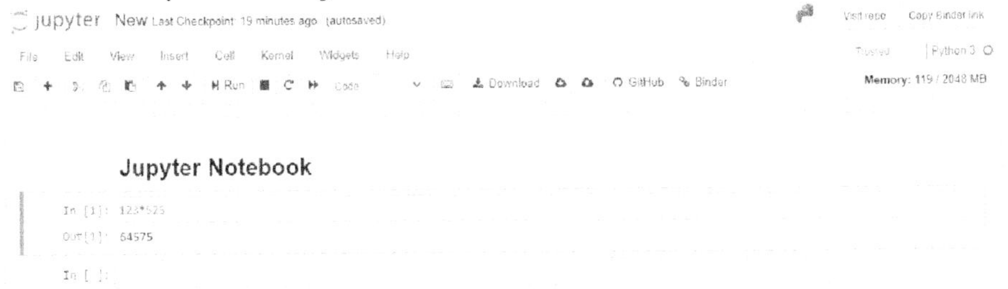

We have more access to the markdown cells, to diplay texts more gracefully. We can add headings, sub-headings and lower-headings, using # 1, 2 and 3 times followed by space and then text respectively.

```
# Jupyter Notebook
## IPython
### Data
```

Jupyter Notebook

IPython

Data

We can create ordered and bulleted lists

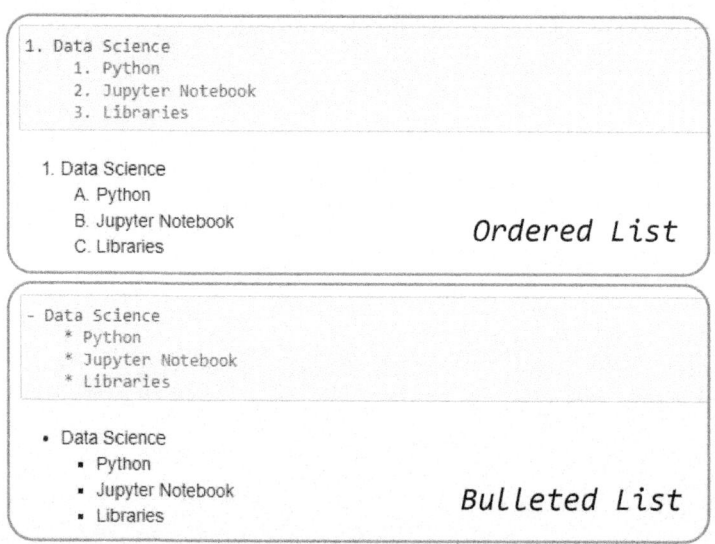

To create an ordered list, use 1 for the first list item and then use tabspace for the sub-list items and use correct numbering. [The text should be written followed by space after the numbers]. To create a bulleted list, use - for square bullets and * for round bullets, and same manner as above for list and sub-list items.

13 SETTING-UP ENVIRONMENT

We can also links, using [] & (). Write the display text in [] and put the link in (), you can also add a hover text inside of ( ) using " " quotes.

```
[Jupter Notebook for Python](https://jupyter.org/try "Try it!")
```

Jupter Notebook for Python

We can also use **<text>** or __<text>__ to render bold text and *<text>* or _<text>_ to render italicized text

```
**Bold** or __BOLD__
```
Bold or **BOLD**

```
*italics* or _italic_
```
italics or *italic*

We can also insert images by going to the Edit>Insert Image and browse your image to enter it

Create tables using | and strictly following the below example

```
|Product|Price|Quantity|
|-------|-----|--------|
|Biscuits|5|2|
|Milk|7|5L|
```

Product	Price	Quantity
Biscuits	5	2
Milk	7	5L

SETTING-UP ENVIRONMENT

Here's a complete list of shortcuts of various operations with cells.

Operations	Shortcut
change cell to code	y
change cell to markdown	m
change cell to raw	r
close the pager	Esc
restart kernal	0 + 0
copy selected cell	c
cut selected cell	x
delete selected cell	d + d
enter edit mode	Enter
extend selection below	Shift + j
extend selection above	Shift + k
find and replace	f
ignore	Shift
insert cell above	a
insert cell below	b
interrupt the kernal	i + i
Merge cells	Shift + m
paste cells above	Shift + v
paste cells below	v
run cell and insert below	Alt + Enter
run cell and select below	Shift + Enter
run selected cells	Ctrl + Enter
save notebook	Ctrl + s
scroll notebook up	SHIFT + Space
scroll notebook down	Space
select all	Ctrl + a
show keyboard shortcuts	h
toggle all line numbers	Shift + l
toggle cell output	o
toggle cell scrolling	Shift + o
toggle line numbers	l
undo cell deletion	z

03 PANADAS LIBRARY

- Features of Pandas library
- Series
- Dataframes

pandas

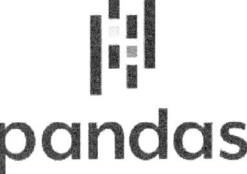

03 PANDAS LIBRARY

Pandas

Data science requires high-performance data manipulation and data analysis, which we can achieve with Pandas Data Structures. Python with pandas is in use in a variety of academic and commercial domains, including Finance, Economics, Statistics, Advertising, Web Analytics, and more. Using Pandas, we can accomplish five typical steps in the processing and analysis of data, regardless of the origin of data — load, organize, manipulate, model, and analyse the data.

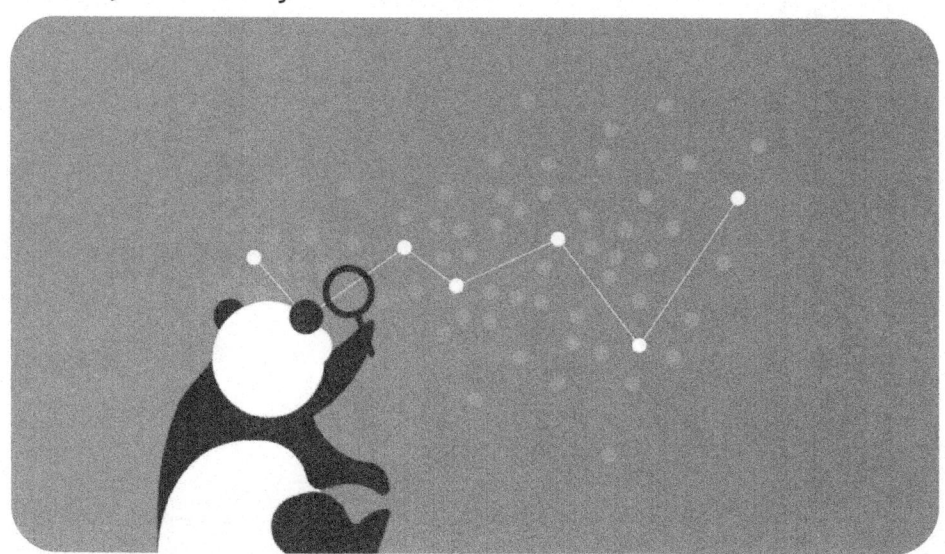

Key features of Pandas library

We can achieve a lot with Pandas library using its features like:
- Fast and efficient DataFrame object with default and customized indexing.
- Tools for loading data into in-memory data objects from different file formats.
- Data alignment and integrated handling of missing data.

17 — PANDAS LIBRARY

- Label-based slicing, indexing and subsetting of large data sets.
- Columns from a data structure can be deleted or inserted.
- Group by data for aggregation and transformations.

Series

Pandas deals with data with it's data structures known as series, data frames and panel. Series is an one-dimensional array like structure with homogeneous data. For example, the following series is a collection of integers

10 17 23 55 67 71 92

As series are homogeneous data structure, it can contain only one type of data [here integer]. So, we conclude that Pandas Series is:
- It is a homogeneous data structure
- Its size cannot be mutated
- Values in series can be mutated

Data Frames

DataFrame is a two-dimensional array with heterogeneous data.

Day	Sales
Monday	33
Tuesday	37
Wednesday	14
Thursday	29

The data shows the sales of certain product for 4 days. You can think of Data Frames a container for 2 or more series. So, we conclude that pandas data frames is:
- It can contain heterogeneous data
- Its size is mutable
- ALso its data is mutable.

We will use Pandas series and data frames a lot in the future lessons, make sure to go through the lesson again and get the grasp of it.

Key Points

- Pandas library is a high performance data manupilation and data analysing tool.
- Pandas data structures include series and data frames
- Series is a 1-Dimensional array of homogeneous data, whose size is immutable but values in a series are mutable.
- Data Frames is a 2-Dimensional array of heterogeneous data of 2 or more series, whose size and data are mutable.

04 NUMPY PACKAGE

- Features of NumPy
- ndarray Objects
- List vs. ndarrays

04 NUMPY PACKAGE

NumPy

NumPy is a Python package which stands for 'Numerical Python'. It is a library consisting of multidimensional array objects and a collection of routines for processing of array.

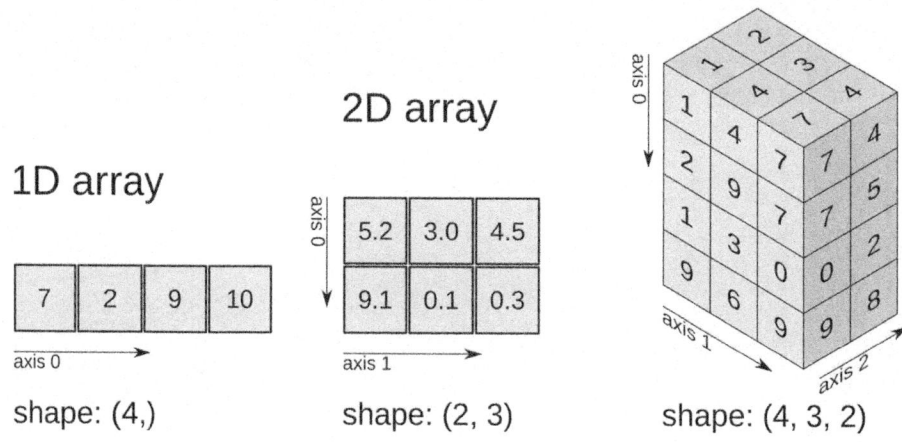

Key features of NumPy

NumPy is powerful that consists of many features like :
- Mathematical and logical operations on arrays.
- Fourier transforms and routines for shape manipulation.
- Operations related to linear algebra. NumPy has in-built functions for linear algebra and random number generation.
- NumPy ndarrays are much much faster than Python Built-in lists and less memoray consuming.
- Most of the part that requires fast computation are written C and C++

ndarray objects

NumPy aims to provide an array object that is up to 50x faster that traditional Python lists. The array object in NumPy is called ndarray, it provides a lot of supporting functions that make working with ndarray very easy. Arrays are very frequently used in data science, where speed and resources are very important.

In NumPy, we can create 0-D,1-D,2-D and 3-D ndarrays.

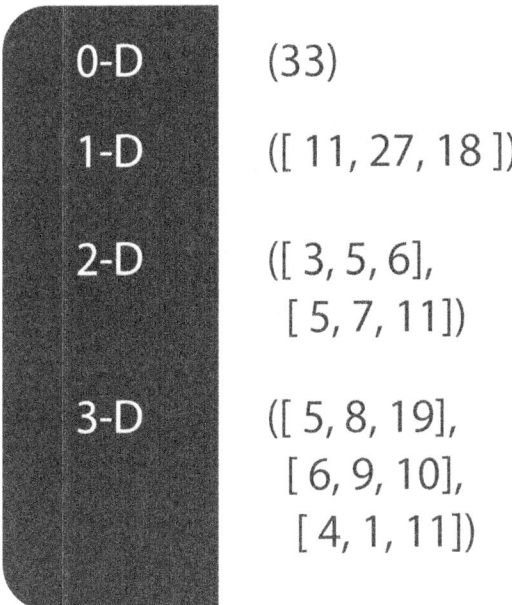

In breif ndarrays or n-dimensional arrays are:
- It describes the collection of items of the same type.
- Items in the collection can be accessed using a zero-based index.
- Every item in an ndarray takes the same size of block in the memory.
- Each element in ndarray is an object of data-type object (called dtype). Any item extracted from ndarray object (by slicing) is represented by a Python object of one of array scalar types.

Lists vs. ndarray

In Python we have lists that serve the purpose of arrays, but they are slow to process. NumPy aims to provide an array object that is up to 50x faster that traditional Python lists.

Lists	ndarrays
• List is an array of heterogeneous objects • List arrays are stored in different places in the memory which, makes it slow to process data. • Lists are not optimized to work with latest CPU's • A 1-Dimensional List ['A',56,67.05]	• ndarray is an array of homogeneous objects • ndarrays arrays are stored in one continuous place in the memory which, makes it faster to process data. • ndarrays are optimized to work with latest CPU's • A 1-Dimensional ndarray ([12, 17, 25])

Lists arrays

PyObject_Head
length
items

0 x 310718
0 x 310719
0 x 310720
0 x 310721
0 x 310722
0 x 310723
0 x 310724

memory loc -12044567
memory loc -12044568
memory loc -12044569
memory loc -12044570
memory loc -12044571
memory loc -12044572
memory loc -12044573
memory loc -12044574
memory loc -12044575
memory loc -12044576
memory loc -12044577
memory loc -12044578

List arrays memory allocation

23 NUMPY PACKAGE

ndarrays

PyObject_Head	1
data	2
dimensions	3
	4
strides	5
	6
	7

ndarrays memory allocation

You can clearly understand why the built-in list arrays are slower than ndarrays.

To accelerate and process data much faster we will use NumPy in future lessons, make sure to geta hold of it.

Key Points

- NumPy stands for Numerical Python, which is a Python Package used for working with arrays.
- It also has functions for working in domain of linear algebra, fourier transform, and matrices.
- ndarrays or n-dimensional arrays are homogeneous arrays, which are optimized for fast processing.
- ndarrays also provide many functions that makes it suitable to work with data

05 SCIPY PACKAGE

- Features of SciPy
- Data Structures
- SciPy Sub-Packages

05 SCIPY PACKAGE

SciPy

The SciPy library of Python is built to work with NumPy arrays and provides many user-friendly and efficient numerical practices such as routines for numerical integration and optimization. Together, they run on all popular operating systems, are quick to install.

```python
In [1]: #Import packages
        from scipy import integrate
        import numpy as np

        def my_integrator(a,b,c):
            my_fun = lambda x: a*np.exp(b*x)+c
            y,err = integrate.quad(my_fun,0,100)
            print('ans: %1.4e, error: %1.4e' % (y,err))
            return(y,err)

        #Call function
        my_integrator (5,-10,3)

        ans: 3.0050e+02, error: 4.5750e-10
Out[1]: (300.5, 4.574965520082099e-10)
```

Key features of SciPy

SciPy combined with NumPy results a powerful tool for data processing with features like:
- The SciPy package contains various toolboxes dedicated to common issues in scientific computing. Its different submodules correspond to different applications, such as interpolation, integration, optimization, image processing, statistics, special functions, etc.
- SciPy is the core package for scientific routines in Python; it is meant to operate efficiently on NumPy arrays, so that numpy and scipy work hand in hand.
- SciPy is organized into sub-packages covering different scientific computing domains, which makes it more efficient.

26 SCIPY PACKAGE

Data structures

The basic data structure used by SciPy is a multidimensional array provided by the NumPy module. NumPy provides some functions for Linear Algebra, Fourier Transforms and Random Number Generation, but not with the generality of the equivalent functions in SciPy. Except for these, SciPy offers Physical and mathematical constants, fourier transform, interpolation, data input and output, sparse metrics, etc.

Dense Matrix

1	2	31	2	9	7	34	22	11	5
11	92	4	3	2	2	3	3	2	1
3	9	13	8	21	17	4	2	1	4
8	32	1	2	34	18	7	78	10	7
9	22	3	9	8	71	12	22	17	3
13	21	21	9	2	47	1	81	21	9
21	12	53	12	91	24	81	8	91	2
61	8	33	82	19	87	16	3	1	55
54	4	78	24	18	11	4	2	99	5
13	22	32	42	9	15	9	22	1	21

Sparse Matrix

1	.	3	.	9	.	3	.	.	.
11	.	4	.	.	.	.	.	2	1
.	.	1	.	.	.	4	.	1	.
8	.	.	.	3	1	.	.	.	.
.	.	.	9	.	.	1	.	17	.
13	21	.	9	2	47	1	81	21	9
.	.	.	.	.	.	.	.	.	.
.	.	.	.	19	8	16	.	.	55
54	4	.	.	.	11	.	.	.	.
.	.	2	.	.	.	.	22	.	21

Use of Sparse matrix

SciPy sub-packages

As we already know, SciPy is organized into sub-packages covering different scientific computing domains, we can import them according to our needs rather than importing the whole library.

The following table shows the list of all the sub-packages of SciPy :
[next page]

27 SCIPY PACKAGE

scipy.constants	Mathematical constants
scipy.fftpack	Fourier transform
scipy.integrate	Integrate routines
scipy.interpolate	Interpolation
scipy.io	Data input and output
scipy.linalg	Linear algebra routines
scipy.optimize	Optimization
scipy.signal	Signal processing
scipy.sparse	Sparse matrices
scipy.spatial	Spatial data structures
scipy.special	Special mathematics
scipy.stats	Statistics

Key Points

- SciPy Package is a toolbox which is used for common scientific issues.
- SciPy together with NumPy creates a dynamic tool for data processing.
- Along with NumPy functions, SciPy provides a lot of functions to perform different tasks with ndarrays.
- SciPy is divided into sub-packages determined for different tasks.

06 MALPLOTLIB LIBRARY

- Features of Matplotlib
- Data Visualization
- PyPlot in Matplotlib

06 MATPLOTLIB LIBRARY

MatPlotLib

Matplotlib is a python library used to create 2D graphs and plots by using python scripts. It has a module named pyplot which makes things easy for plotting by providing feature to control line styles, font properties, formatting axes etc.

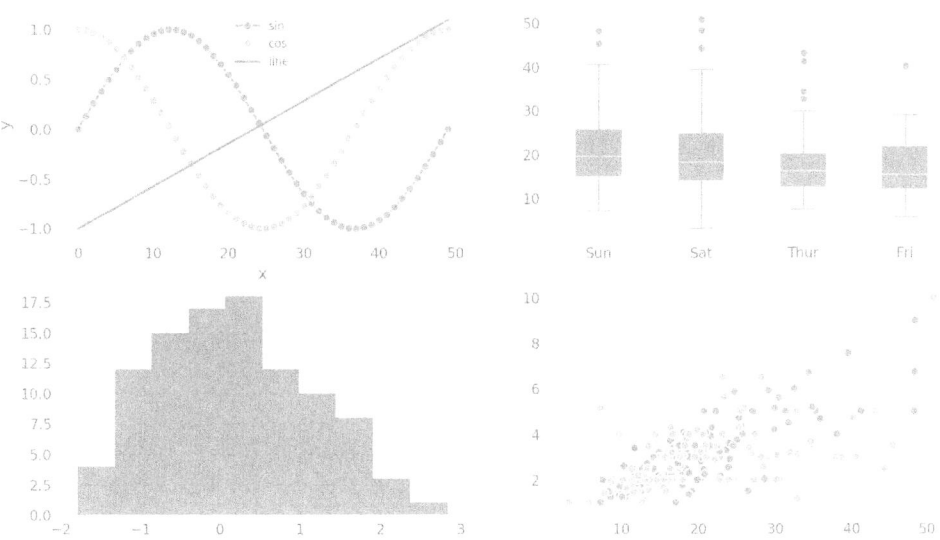

Key features of MatPlotLib

Matplotlib is the best choice for data visualization because of its features like:
- It supports a very wide variety of graphs and plots namely - histogram, bar charts, power spectra, error charts, and many more.
- It is used along with NumPy to provide an environment that is an effective open source alternative for MatLab.
- Using its PyPlot module, plotting simple graphs or any other charts is very easy.

Data Visualization

Data visualization is the graphical representation of information and data. By using visual elements like charts, graphs, and maps, data visualization tools provide an accessible way to see and understand trends, outliers, and patterns in data.

In the world of Big Data, data visualization tools and technologies are essential to analyze massive amounts of information and make data-driven decisions. Data visulaization helps us to view data in a graphical or more interesting way rather than viewing a big chunk of numbers in a uniform line.

We will process, analyze and then visualize our data, if we don't visualize our data, it loose a lot of impact as it will in the form bar graphs, pie charts, etc.

PyPlot in Matplotlib

`matplotlib.pyplot` is a collection of functions that make matplotlib work like MATLAB. Each pyplot function makes some change to a figure: e.g., creates a figure, creates a plotting area in a figure, plots some lines in a plotting area, decorates the plot with labels, etc.

To test it yourself, jump to Jupyter Notebook and start of by importing the `matplotlib.pyplot` module.

```
In [ ]: import matplotlib.pyplot as mplt
```

To plot a simple graph, use the `plot` function and pass a list, and then use the `show` function to view the graph

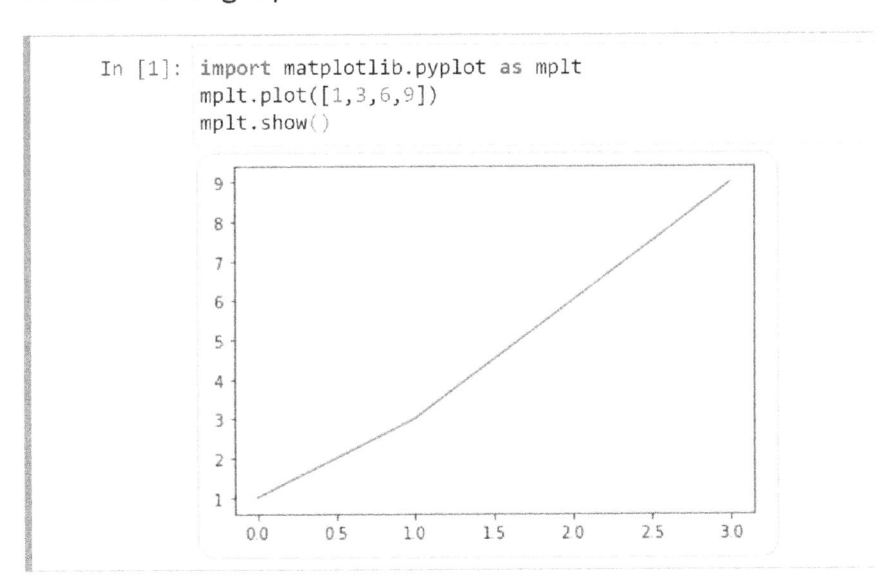

```
In [1]: import matplotlib.pyplot as mplt
        mplt.plot([1,3,6,9])
        mplt.show()
```

We have successfully plotted our graph with some random values in a list.

If we want we can name x and y axis using the `xlabel` and `ylabel` repectively.

MATPLOTLIB LIBRARY

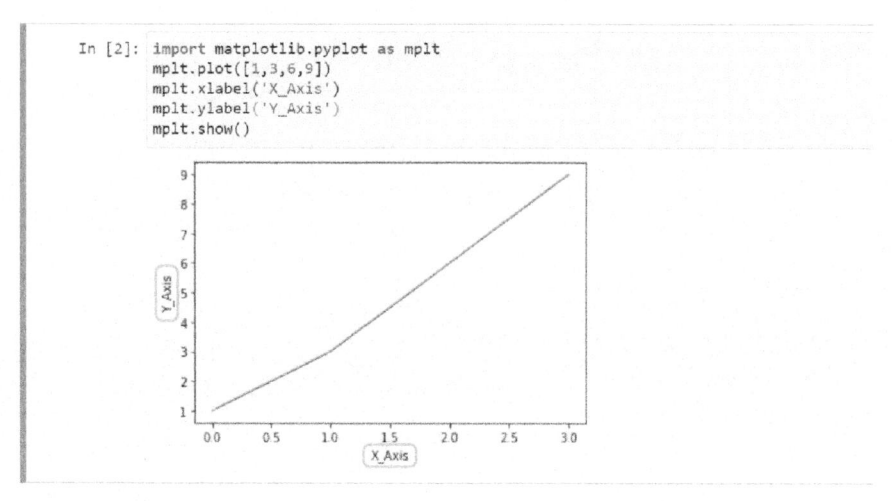

```
In [2]: import matplotlib.pyplot as mplt
        mplt.plot([1,3,6,9])
        mplt.xlabel('X_Axis')
        mplt.ylabel('Y_Axis')
        mplt.show()
```

The graph has solid blue line, we change it's color and the line style by passing another argument to the plot function like, 'ro' for 'r' red and 'o' circles.

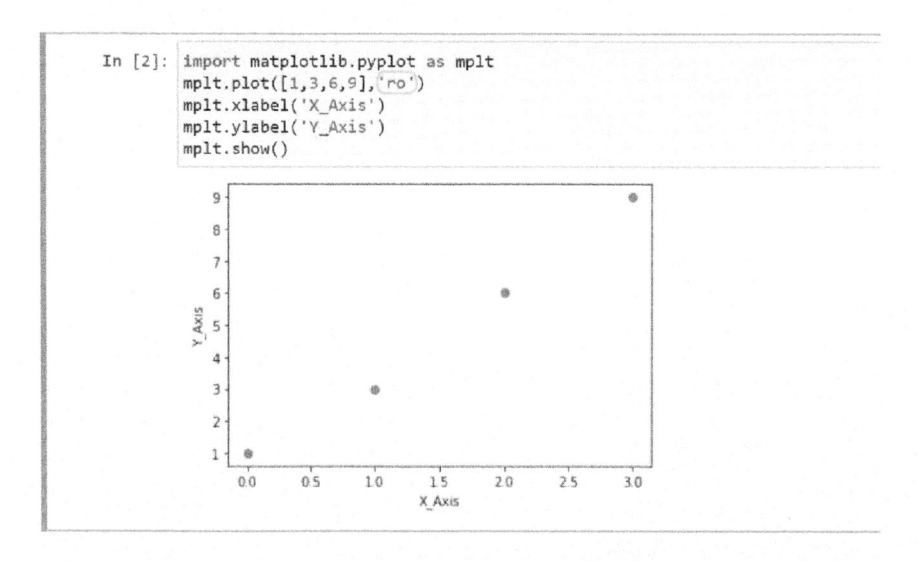

```
In [2]: import matplotlib.pyplot as mplt
        mplt.plot([1,3,6,9],'ro')
        mplt.xlabel('X_Axis')
        mplt.ylabel('Y_Axis')
        mplt.show()
```

The letters and symbols of the format string like 'ro' are from MATLAB, and you concatenate a color string with a line style string. There are many symbols for different shapes and colors like, 'b-' for blue solid. You'll find all the symbols for different color and shapes in the following list.

MATPLOTLIB LIBRARY

line and shape styles

`-`	Solid line
`--`	Dashed line
`:`	Dotted line
`-.`	Dash-Dot line
`'o'`	Circle
`'+'`	Plus sign
`'*'`	Asterisk
`'.'`	Point
`'x'`	Cross
`'_'`	Horizontal line
`'|'`	Vertical line
`'s'`	Square
`'d'`	Diamond
`'^'`	Upward-pointing triangle
`'v'`	Downward-pointing triangle
`'>'`	Right-pointing triangle
`'<'`	Left-pointing triangle
`'p'`	Pentagram
`'h'`	Hexagram

color styles

y	yellow
m	magenta
c	cyan
r	red
g	green
b	blue
w	white
k	black

MATPLOTLIB LIBRARY

Except for the color and line & shape style we have a lot of editibility on the plotted graphs, which we will discover in the future lessons.

Key Points

- MatPlotLib is a library used for visualizing our data using it's MATLAB like functions
- MatPlotLib's PyPlot module makes it easier to plot data, with full control over color, line & shape, font, axis-labels, etc.
- It supports wide range of graphs and plots like, histogram, bar graphs, pie charts, and even 3-D graphs.
- MatPlotLib is the best library for data visualization

07 DATA OPERATION AND CLEANSING

- Data Processing
- Numpy Operations
- Pandas Operations
- Slicing Syntax
- More with ndarrays
- Data Cleansing

07 DATA OPERATIONS AND CLEANSING

Data Processing

Python handles data of various formats mainly through the two libraries, Pandas and Numpy. We have already seen the important features of these two libraries in the previous chapters. In this chapter we will see some basic examples from each of the libraries on how to operate on data.

NumPy Operations

To start working with NumPy, we need to import `numpy` to create NumPy arrays.

```
In [ ]: import numpy
```

Now let's create an array, using the `array` function and print it.

```
In [2]: import numpy
        ar = numpy.array([1,5,7])
        print(ar)

        [1 5 7]
```

`ar` is a 1-Dimensional array, we can also create a 2-Dimensional array by creating one or more 1-Dimensional array inside of another array

```
In [8]: import numpy
        ar = numpy.array([[1,5,7], [2,3,9]])
        print(ar)

        [[1 5 7]
         [2 3 9]]
```

```
[[1 5 7]         ──── 1-D array
 [2 3 9]]        ──── 2-D array
```

We can specify the dimension of an array during creation using the `ndmin` parameter

```
In [10]: import numpy
         ar = numpy.array([1,5,7], ndmin = 2 )
         print(ar)

         [[1 5 7]]
```

Although we passed a 1-Dimensional array, it became a 2-Dimensional array because of the specification of the dimensions of the array in the `ndmin` parameter

We created an array with integers so, let's create arrays with strings and floats using the `dtype` parameter with the same values

```
In [11]: import numpy
         ar_str = numpy.array([1,5,7], dtype = str )
         ar_flt = numpy.array([1,5,7], dtype = float)
         print(ar_str)
         print(ar_flt)

         ['1' '5' '7']
         [1. 5. 7.]
```

`ar_str` is an array of string literals and `ar_flt` is an array of floats. We can also change these numbers to complex numbers the same way using complex as `dtype`

```
In [13]: import numpy
         ar_str = numpy.array([1,5,7], dtype = str )
         ar_flt = numpy.array([1,5,7], dtype = float)
         ar_cmx = numpy.array([1,5,7], dtype = complex )
         print(ar_str)
         print(ar_flt)
         print(ar_cmx)

         ['1' '5' '7']
         [1. 5. 7.]
         [1.+0.j 5.+0.j 7.+0.j]
```

`ar_str`, `ar_flt` and `ar_cmx` are arrays created with same data, but with different data types as strings, floats and complex numbers repectively.

Pandas Operations

Pandas handles data through Series, Data Frame, and Panel. We will learn to create each of these.

Pandas Series

We already know what Pandas Series is. A pandas Series can be created using the Series function so, let's import pandas and create series.

```
In [14]: import pandas
         sr = pandas.Series([1,5,7])
         print(sr)

         0    1
         1    5
         2    7
         dtype: int64
```

As you can see our data is indexed form 0 to 2 with the data type printed as integer, we can specify our own indexes in the `index` parameter

```
In [16]: import pandas
         sr = pandas.Series([1,5,7], index = ['A','B','C'])
         print(sr)

         A    1
         B    5
         C    7
         dtype: int64
```

Like ndarrays, we can also specify the data type in pandas series using `dtype` parameter during series creation

```
In [18]: import pandas
         sr = pandas.Series([1,5,7], dtype = complex )
         print(sr)

         0    1.000000+0.000000j
         1    5.000000+0.000000j
         2    7.000000+0.000000j
         dtype: complex128
```

We can use a ndarray to create a pandas series

```
In [19]: import numpy
         import pandas
         ar = numpy.array([1,5,7])
         sr = pandas.Series( data = ar, copy = True )
         #is same as sr = pandas.series(ar, copy = True)
         print(sr)

         0    1
         1    5
         2    7
         dtype: int32
```

We passed the `ar` ndarray as the data for the series [use of the `data` parameter isn't necessary, its just for better understanding] and also used the `copy` parameter to create a copy of the data.

If you want to get the data, without the indexes use the `values` function

```
In [21]: import numpy
         import pandas
         ar = numpy.array([1,5,7])
         sr = pandas.Series(ar)
         print(sr.values)

         [1 5 7]
```

You can print a more detailed version of the above using the `array` function

```
In [22]: import numpy
         import pandas
         ar = numpy.array([1,5,7])
         sr = pandas.Series(ar)
         print(sr.array)

         <PandasArray>
         [1, 5, 7]
         Length: 3, dtype: int32
```

<PandasArray> — Array Type
[1, 5, 7] — values
Length: 3, dtype: int32 — data type
length

You can use `values` or `array` function according to your needs whether you want just the values or summarized detail of the arrays in that panda series. Also note the difference in the `array` function in NumPy and Pandas.

Pandas Data Frames

Pandas Data Frames aligns data in a tabular fashion of rows and columns. A pandas DataFrame can be created using the `DataFrame` function, we need pass a dictionary as the data

```
In [23]: import pandas
         df = pandas.DataFrame({"Product":['Cookies','Biscuits'],
                                "Sales":[157,227]})
         print(df)

             Product  Sales
         0   Cookies    157
         1  Biscuits    227
```

Dictionary keys are the columns and their values are the content of the rows of the Data Frame. We can also use `index` parameter here

```
In [24]: import pandas
         df = pandas.DataFrame({"Product":['Cookies','Biscuits'],
                                "Sales":[157,227]}, index = [1,2])
         print(df)

             Product  Sales
         1   Cookies    157
         2  Biscuits    227
```

We can define the columns and it's data seperately using ndarrays

```
In [42]: import pandas
         import numpy
         ar = numpy.array([[1,3],[6,2]])

         df = pandas.DataFrame(data = ar,
                               index = ['A','B'],
                               columns = ['C1','C2'])
         print(df)

            C1  C2
         A   1   3
         B   6   2
```

The data is stored in the ndarray and the columns are defined in the DataFrame's `columns` parameter. Note that, a 2-Dimensional ndarray with 2 1-Dimensional arrays in it is passed to the `data` parameter to act as the data

DATA OPERATIONS & CLEANSING

We can add columns to the DataFrame using the `<DataFrame>[<column_name>] = <values>` syntax

```
In [44]: import pandas
         import numpy
         ar = numpy.array([[1,3],[6,2]])

         df = pandas.DataFrame(data = ar,
                              index = ['A','B'],
                              columns = ['C1','C2'])
         df['C3'] = (df['C1']*5)
         print(df)

            C1  C2  C3
         A   1   3   5
         B   6   2  30
```

We can delete columns from the DataFrame using the `del` function

```
In [45]: import pandas
         import numpy
         ar = numpy.array([[1,3],[6,2]])

         df = pandas.DataFrame(data = ar,
                              index = ['A','B'],
                              columns = ['C1','C2'])
         df['C3'] = (df['C1']*5)
         del df['C2']
         print(df)

            C1  C3
         A   1   5
         B   6  30
```

We can print a column of the DataFrame using the `<DataFrame>[<column_name>]` syntax

```
In [46]: import pandas
         import numpy
         ar = numpy.array([[1,3],[6,2]])

         df = pandas.DataFrame(data = ar,
                              index = ['A','B'],
                              columns = ['C1','C2'])
         print(df['C1'])

         A    1
         B    6
         Name: C1, dtype: int32
```

41 | DATA OPERATIONS & CLEANSING

Slicing Syntax

To get a single element from a ndarray or pandas series or pandas dataframes, we need to use the slice syntax <array>[start:end:step(optional)]

Let's extract some elements from the arrays we have created so far.

```
In [59]: import numpy as npy
         ar1 = npy.array([1, 5])
         ar2 = npy.array([[1, 3],
                          [5, 2]])
         ar3 = npy.array([[[1, 3],
                           [5, 2]],
                          [[2, 4],
                           [4, 6]]])

         #Slicing 1-Dimensional array
         print(ar1[0])

         #Slicing 2-Dimensional array
         print(ar2[0,1])

         #Slicing 3-Dimensional array
         print(ar3[1,0,1])

         1
         3
         4
```

We use a comma , to slice further in 2 or more dimensional arrays, the following figure will help you understand the slicing of the 3-Dimensional array more better

ar3[] ⟶ [[[1, 3],
          [5, 2]],
         [[2, 4],
          [4, 6]]]

Full array

42 DATA OPERATIONS & CLEANSING

ar3[1]   [[[1, 3],
                                  [5, 2]],
                                 [[2, 4],
                                  [4, 6]]]

First Slice

ar3[1,0]   [[[1, 3],
                                  [5, 2]],
                                 [[2, 4],
                                  [4, 6]]]

Second Slice

ar3[1,0,1]   [[[1, 3],
                                  [5, 2]],
                                 [[2, 4],
                                  [4, 6]]]

ar3[1,0,1]   4

Final Slice

 Slicing may seem a bit tough for beginners due to the dimensions, that's why I created the figure to help you understand slicing better. If you are confident try solving the slicing questions in the Exercise

DATA OPERATIONS & CLEANSING

To get a element from a pandas series, we use the `<series>[<explicit_index> or <implicit_index>]` syntax

```
In [4]: import pandas as pan
        sr = pan.Series([1, 3, 5], index = ['a','b','c'])

        print(sr['a']) #implicit indexing
        print(sr[0])   #explicit indexing

        1
        1
```

If you have indexes like numbers like these

```
In [6]: import pandas as pan
        sr = pan.Series([1, 3, 5], index = [2,4,6])
```

If you want the second element using the implicit index [indexing defined in index parameter] use `<series>.loc[<label>]` syntax and using the explicit indexing [0,1,2,...] use `<series>.iloc[<index>]` syntax

```
In [7]: import pandas as pan
        sr = pan.Series([1, 3, 5], index = [2,4,6])

        print(sr.loc[4])
        print(sr.iloc[1])

        3
        3
```

We can modify or delete the elements using slicing

```
In [9]: import pandas as pan
        sr = pan.Series([1, 3, 5], index = [2,4,6])

        sr[4] = 7
        print(sr)

        del sr[6]
        print(sr)

        2    1
        4    7
        6    5
        dtype: int64
        2    1
        4    7
        dtype: int64
```

Let's say we have a DataFrame like this

```
In [27]: import pandas as pan
         sr = pan.DataFrame({'Product':['Biscuit','Cookies'],
                             'Sales':[227,158]}, index = [1,2])
         sr

Out[27]:
            Product  Sales
         1  Biscuit    227
         2  Cookies    158
```

And want the Sales Column only, so use the `<DataFrame>[<column_label>]` syntax

```
In [32]: import pandas as pan
         sr = pan.DataFrame({'Product':['Biscuit','Cookies'],
                             'Sales':[227,158]}, index = [1,2])
         sr['Sales']

Out[32]: 1    227
         2    158
         Name: Sales, dtype: int64
```

or to get the second row only, so use the `<DataFrame>.loc[<row_index>]` syntax

```
In [33]: import pandas as pan
         sr = pan.DataFrame({'Product':['Biscuit','Cookies'],
                             'Sales':[227,158]}, index = [1,2])
         sr.loc[2] #You can also use sr.iloc[1]

Out[33]: Product    Cookies
         Sales          158
         Name: 2, dtype: object
```

or to get the sales of cookies only, so use the `<DataFrame>.values[<index>]` syntax

```
In [37]: import pandas as pan
         sr = pan.DataFrame({'Product':['Biscuit','Cookies'],
                             'Sales':[227,158]}, index = [1,2])
         sr.values[1,1]

Out[37]: 158
```

The values are stored as ndarrays, that's why it used slicing similar to that of 2-Dimensional ndarrays

We can delete a whole column from the DataFrame

```
In [41]: import pandas as pan
         sr = pan.DataFrame({'Product':['Biscuit','Cookies'],
                             'Sales':[227,158]}, index = [1,2])
         sr
```

Out[41]:

	Product	Sales
1	Biscuit	227
2	Cookies	158

```
In [45]: del sr['Sales']
         sr
```

Out[45]:

	Product
1	Biscuit
2	Cookies

but we cannot delete a value

```
In [47]: import pandas as pan
         sr = pan.DataFrame({'Product':['Biscuit','Cookies'],
                             'Sales':[227,158]}, index = [1,2])
         del sr.values[1,1]
---------------------------------------------------------------------------
ValueError                                Traceback (most recent call last)
<ipython-input-47-4422f0e71c59> in <module>
      2 sr = pan.DataFrame({'Product':['Biscuit','Cookies'],
      3                     'Sales':[227,158]}, index = [1,2])
----> 4 del sr.values[1,1]

ValueError: cannot delete array elements
```

nor you can modify a value

```
In [48]: import pandas as pan
         sr = pan.DataFrame({'Product':['Biscuit','Cookies'],
                             'Sales':[227,158]}, index = [1,2])
         sr
```

Out[48]:

	Product	Sales
1	Biscuit	227
2	Cookies	158

```
In [51]: sr.values[1,1] = 162
         sr.values[1,1]
```

Out[51]: 158

More with ndarrays

We can reverse a ndarray using `<array>[::-1]` syntax

```
In [56]: import numpy as npy
         ar = npy.array([1,2,3,4])
         ar

Out[56]: array([1, 2, 3, 4])
```

```
In [55]: ar = ar[::-1]
         ar

Out[55]: array([4, 3, 2, 1])
```

We can broadcast a whole ndarray without doing it the long way

```
In [56]: import numpy as npy
         ar = npy.array([1,2,3,4])
         ar

Out[56]: array([1, 2, 3, 4])
```

```
In [62]: # the long way - ar + [1,1,1,1]
         ar = ar + 1
         ar

Out[62]: array([2, 3, 4, 5])
```

We can sort an array with the `sort` function

```
In [63]: import numpy as npy
         ar = npy.array([5,1,3,9])
         ar

Out[63]: array([5, 1, 3, 9])
```

```
In [64]: ar.sort()
         ar

Out[64]: array([1, 3, 5, 9])
```

There are many built-in ndarray methods that will not be discussed now, but will be used in the future lessons in various steps, you may go to the documentation to find all the functions and their roles, as we don't require every function for our data processing and analyzing, all the miscellaneous functions are not discussed in this book

Data Cleansing

Let's consider a situtation like below

```
In [71]:  import pandas as pan
          import numpy as npy
          ar = npy.array([[1,2,3],[4,7,2],[4,9,1]])
          df = pan.DataFrame( data = ar, index = ['a','c','e'],
                              columns = ['C1','C2','C3'])
          df
```

Out[71]:

	C1	C2	C3
a	1	2	3
c	4	7	2
e	4	9	1

```
In [72]:  df = df.reindex(['a','b','c','d','e'])
          df
```

Out[72]:

	C1	C2	C3
a	1.0	2.0	3.0
b	NaN	NaN	NaN
c	4.0	7.0	2.0
d	NaN	NaN	NaN
e	4.0	9.0	1.0

The reindexed Data Frame has NaN values in the b and d rows. This happened because, there is no data for b and d rows. Using reindexing, we have created a DataFrame with missing values. In the output, NaN means Not a Number. To make detecting missing values easier (and across different array dtypes), Pandas provides the `isnull()` and `notnull()` functions, which are also methods on Series and DataFrame objects

```
In [73]:  df['C1'].isnull()
```

Out[73]:
```
a    False
b    True
c    False
d    True
e    False
Name: C1, dtype: bool
```

48 DATA OPERATIONS & CLEANSING

Pandas provides various methods for cleaning the missing values. The fillna function can `fillna` NaN values with non-null data in a couple of ways like replacing NaN values with 0

```
In [74]: df.fillna(0)
Out[74]:
     C1   C2   C3
a   1.0  2.0  3.0
b   0.0  0.0  0.0
c   4.0  7.0  2.0
d   0.0  0.0  0.0
e   4.0  9.0  1.0
```

We can copy the value above or below that data using `pad` or `bfill` in method parameter of `fillna` function

```
In [75]: df.fillna( method = 'pad' )
Out[75]:
     C1   C2   C3
a   1.0  2.0  3.0
b   1.0  2.0  3.0
c   4.0  7.0  2.0
d   4.0  7.0  2.0
e   4.0  9.0  1.0
```

We can drop the rows with missing values with `dropna` function

```
In [76]: df.dropna()
Out[76]:
     C1   C2   C3
a   1.0  2.0  3.0
c   4.0  7.0  2.0
e   4.0  9.0  1.0
```

DATA OPERATIONS & CLEANSING

If we want to change a single value in a Data Frame, we can use the `replace` function

```
In [78]: import pandas as pan
         import numpy as npy
         ar = npy.array([[1,2,3],[4,7,2],[4,9,1]])
         df = pan.DataFrame( data = ar, index = ['a','c','e'],
                             columns = ['C1','C2','C3'])
         df.replace({3:13})
```

Out[78]:

	C1	C2	C3
a	1	2	13
c	4	7	2
e	4	9	1

Key Points

- We can create ndarrays using the `array` function.
- We can slice ndarrays using the `<array>[<index>,<index>, ... ]` syntax
- We can broadcast ndarrays directly using `<array> += <number>` syntax
- We can create Pandas Series using the `Series` function, which takes `data[values]`, `index[specify indexing]`, `dtype[specify the the data type]` and `copy[whether or not copy the data]` as parameters.
- We can create Pandas DataFrames using the `DataFrame` function, which takes `data[dict]`, `index[specify indexing]`, `dtype[specify the the data type]`, `columns[labels of the columns]` and `copy[whether or not copy the data]` as parameters.
- We can slice Pandas Series and DataFrames using `<variable>[<index> or <column_name>]`

EXERCISE

Q1. Create a ndarray with the data of the precipitation in a week:
 12mm 14mm 7mm 0mm 3mm 21mm 10mm
store this array in a precipitation_data variable and print a sorted list.

Q2. Create a Pandas Series with the above data and index them as:
 Mon Tue Wed Thu Fri Sat Sun
and print it.

Q3. Create a Pandas Series with the given data
 10 45 60 12 40
and perform the following tasks:
- index them from 'A' to 'E'
- Change the 'B' value to 65
- delete the 'E' Value
- print the Series

Q4. Create a Pandas DataFrame with the given data
 Subjects : Maths, Science, Literature, Comp.Sci.
 Marks   : 75,94,88,97
create appropriate columns and indexes then perform the following tasks:
- index them from '1' to '4'
- add 'Physical Education' : 95 to the DataFrame
- change the value of Math's Marks to 81
- reindex the DataFrame with the subjects [Maths, Sci,...]
- delete the Subjects column
- print the DataFrame

Q4. Create a ar1 ndarray with data of first 10 even numbers and another ar2 ndarray with the data of first 10 odd numbers. Then create a Pandas DataFrame using the ar1 and ar2 as data, and label the columns as Even and Odd and index them in roman numbers
[i, ii, iii, iv, v, ...] Display the result

51 EXERCISE

Q5. Without running the code yourself, try finding the output for the following Code Cells

```
In [9]: import numpy as npy

        ar = npy.array([[["a","b","e"],["x","y","d"]],
                        [["v","l","g"],["k","m","o"]]])
        num1 = ar[0,1,0]
        num2 = ar[0,1,1]
        num3 = ar[1,1,1]

        print(num1, num2, num3)
```

```
In [12]: import numpy as npy

         ar = npy.array([[[1,3,5,1],[8,2,9,0]],
                         [[3,5,2,9],[2,7,0,3]]])
         num1 = ar[1,0,2]
         num2 = ar[0,0,0]
         num3 = ar[1,1,1]
         num4 = ar[0,1,2]

         print(num1, num2, num3, num4)
```

```
In [23]: import pandas as pan
         import numpy as npy
         ar = npy.array([[1,2,3],[5,9,7]])
         df = pan.DataFrame(ar, columns = ["C1","C2","C3"],
                           index = ['R1','R2'])

         print(df['C1'])
         print(df.loc['R2'])
         print(df.iloc[0])
         print(df.values[0,2])
```

Hint: You may go over the pages 44-45 again if you can't find the answer. Check your answers by running the code.

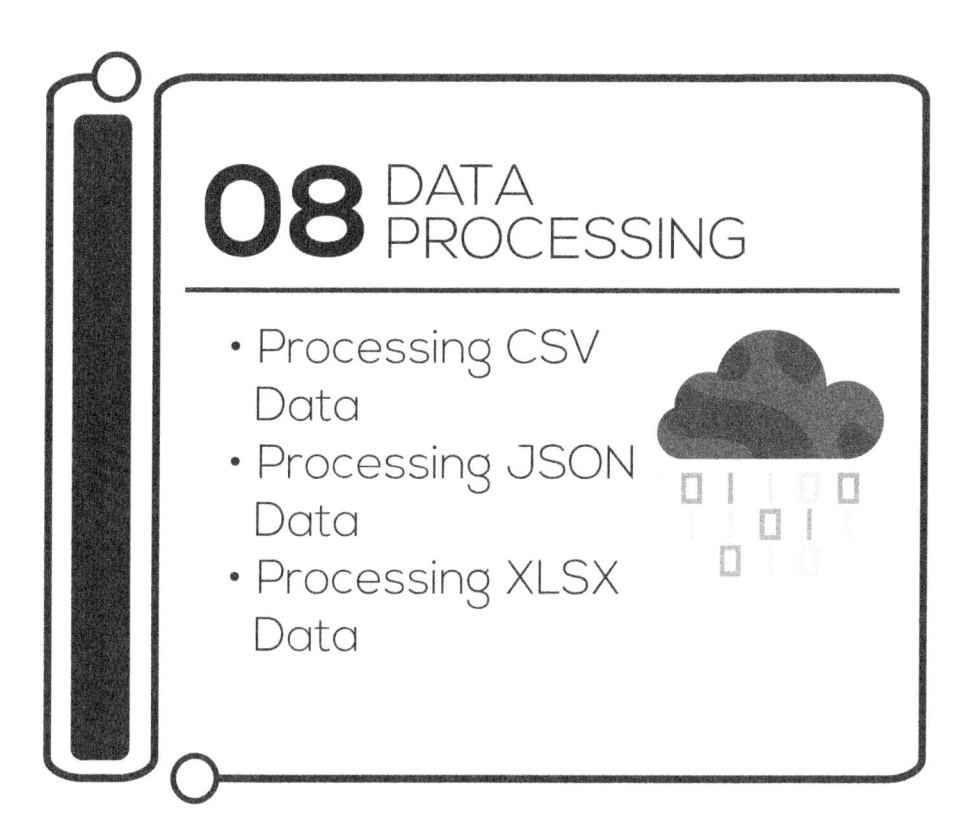

08 DATA PROCESSING

- Processing CSV Data
- Processing JSON Data
- Processing XLSX Data

08 DATA PROCESSING

Data Processing

Often we have data in multiple file formats like, data of sales of any product, number of subscribers, etc. We will use Pandas library to import different data files

Processing CSV Data

Reading data from CSV(comma separated values) is a fundamental necessity in Data Science. Often, we get data from various sources which can get exported to CSV format so that they can be used by other systems. To work with csv files we need one first, you can download the sample file from here
http://bit.ly/csv_dt
To import it, you need move the csv file in the place where your Jupyter Notebook is hosted, to find it use the below code

```
In [32]: import os
         print(os.getcwd())

         C:\Users\Rahul
```

Move your file there, and use the `read_csv` function of pandas library to import the csv file

```
In [38]: import pandas as pan
         dt = pan.read_csv("csv_data.csv")
         dt
```

Out[38]:

	id	name	price	sales	brand
0	101	biscuits	5.00	227	HomeFoods
1	102	cookies	7.25	158	TBakery
2	103	cake	12.00	50	TBakery
3	104	whey_supplement	34.90	24	MusleUp
4	105	protein_bars	4.90	85	MusleUp
5	106	potato_chips	1.75	121	HomeFoods

DATA PROCESSING

We can access a single column of the csv data using slicing like DataFrames

```
In [39]: import pandas as pan
         dt = pan.read_csv("csv_data.csv")
         dt['sales']

Out[39]: 0    227
         1    158
         2     50
         3     24
         4     85
         5    121
         Name: sales, dtype: int64
```

We can extract only 2 or more columns from the data using the `loc[:,[<*columns>]]` function

```
In [44]: import pandas as pan
         dt = pan.read_csv("csv_data.csv")
         dt.loc[:,['name','sales']]

Out[44]:
```

	name	sales
0	biscuits	227
1	cookies	158
2	cake	50
3	whey_supplement	24
4	protein_bars	85
5	potato_chips	121

or just with some rows

```
In [46]: import pandas as pan
         dt = pan.read_csv("csv_data.csv")
         dt.loc[4:6,['name','sales']]

Out[46]:
```

	name	sales
4	protein_bars	85
5	potato_chips	121

DATA PROCESSING

To access a single element, we can use its row-column index with the `values` function

In [49]:
```
import pandas as pan
dt = pan.read_csv("csv_data.csv")
dt
```

Out[49]:

	id	name	price	sales	brand
0	101	biscuits	5.00	227	HomeFoods
1	102	cookies	7.25	158	TBakery
2	103	cake	12.00	50	TBakery
3	104	whey_supplement	34.90	24	MusleUp
4	105	protein_bars	4.90	85	MusleUp
5	106	potato_chips	1.75	121	HomeFoods

In [50]:
```
biscuits_sales = dt.values[0,3]
biscuits_sales
```

Out[50]: 227

	0	1	2	3	4
	id	name	price	sales	brand
0	101	biscuits	5.00	227	HomeFoods
1	102	cookies	7.25	158	TBakery
2	103	cake	12.00	50	TBakery
3	104	whey_supplement	34.90	24	MusleUp
4	105	protein_bars	4.90	85	MusleUp
5	106	potato_chips	1.75	121	HomeFoods

`dt.values`

`dt.values[0]`

`dt.values[0,3]`

`dt.values[0,3]` → `227`

The data values are stored as ndarrays so, to access single elements we can using slicing similar to that of DataFrames

Processing JSON Data

JSON file stores data as text in human-readable format. JSON stands for JavaScript Object Notation. Get your sample JSON data here
http://bit.ly/json_data Pandas can read JSON files using the `read_json` function

```
In [2]: import pandas as pan
        dt = pan.read_json("json_data.json")
        dt
```

Out[2]:

	ID	Name	Price	Sales	Brand
0	101	Biscuits	5.00	227	HomeFoods
1	102	Cookies	7.25	158	TBakery
2	103	Cake	12.00	52	TBakery
3	104	Whey Supplement	34.90	24	MusleUp
4	105	Protein Bars	4.90	85	MusleUp
5	106	Potato Chips	1.75	121	HomeFoods

Similar to the CSV files, we can perform all the slicing and data extraction with JSON data files

```
In [6]: import pandas as pan
        dt = pan.read_json("json_data.json")
        print(dt.loc[:,["ID","Name","Sales"]])
        print(dt["Name"])
        print(dt.values[5,4])
```

```
    ID              Name  Sales
0  101          Biscuits    227
1  102           Cookies    158
2  103              Cake     52
3  104   Whey Supplement     24
4  105      Protein Bars     85
5  106      Potato Chips    121
0            Biscuits
1             Cookies
2                Cake
3     Whey Supplement
4        Protein Bars
5        Potato Chips
Name: Name, dtype: object
HomeFoods
```

57 DATA PROCESSING

Processing XLSX Data

Microsoft Excel is a very widely used spread sheet program. Its user friendliness and appealing features makes it a very frequently used tool in Data Science. Get your sample JSON data here
http://bit.ly/xlsx_data

The `read_excel` function of the pandas library is used read the content of an Excel file into the python environment as a pandas DataFrame.

```
In [9]: import pandas as pan
        dt = pan.read_excel("xlsx_data.xlsx")
        dt
```

Out[9]:

	id	name	price	sales	brand	Unnamed: 5
0	101	biscuits	5.00	227	HomeFoods	NaN
1	102	cookies	7.25	158	TBakery	NaN
2	103	cake	12.00	50	34	TBakery
3	104	whey_supplement	34.90	24	MusleUp	NaN
4	105	protein_bars	4.90	85	MusleUp	NaN
5	106	potato_chips	1.75	121	HomeFoods	NaN

As execel sheets are imported as Pandas DataFrames, we can perform all the tasks on the excel data like Data Frames.

You may notice, we have a `Unnamed: 5` column with `NaN` values [except `dt.value[2,5]`]. Let's clean up our data.

First we need to remove the `Unnamed: 5` column, which we can do using the `del` keyword

```
In [10]: import pandas as pan
         dt = pan.read_excel("xlsx_data.xlsx")
         del dt["Unnamed: 5"]
```

As we have learned earlier the `del` keyword removes the whole column we don't need to deal with the Data Cleansing

DATA PROCESSING

We have removed the Unnamed: 5 column

```
In [11]: import pandas as pan
         dt = pan.read_excel("xlsx_data.xlsx")
         del dt["Unnamed: 5"]
         dt
```

Out[11]:

	id	name	price	sales	brand
0	101	biscuits	5.00	227	HomeFoods
1	102	cookies	7.25	158	TBakery
2	103	cake	12.00	50	34
3	104	whey_supplement	34.90	24	MusleUp
4	105	protein_bars	4.90	85	MusleUp
5	106	potato_chips	1.75	121	HomeFoods

Now, we need to replace dt.value[2,5] i.e. 34 with TBakery. We can use the replace method

```
In [12]: import pandas as pan
         dt = pan.read_excel("xlsx_data.xlsx")
         del dt["Unnamed: 5"]
         dt.replace({34:"TBakery"})
```

Out[12]:

	id	name	price	sales	brand
0	101	biscuits	5.00	227	HomeFoods
1	102	cookies	7.25	158	TBakery
2	103	cake	12.00	50	TBakery
3	104	whey_supplement	34.90	24	MusleUp
4	105	protein_bars	4.90	85	MusleUp
5	106	potato_chips	1.75	121	HomeFoods

So our data is clean with no errors. Try recaping the chapter and attempt the Exercise, where you'll be provided with sample data files [links] with lots of errors and you have to perform all the data cleansing practised in the previous lesson, this will be a very good exercise to help you understand about data processing and cleansing more

DATA PROCESSING

Key Points

- We can import different data files using Pandas library.
- We can import CSV files with the pandas `read_csv` function
- We can import JSON files with the pandas `read_json` function
- We can import Microsoft Excel files with the pandas `read_excel` function

EXERCISE

Q1. Download the following CSV data file
dropgalaxy.in/4icnfgkhghnf
and import it and do the following tasks with data:
- create another copy of the data in `dta` with only 6 columns and 10 rows from the above data
- display the data
- in the `Gender` column, format F to Female and M to Male
- display the data
- remove the `Emp ID` and `Middle initial` columns
- display the data
- create a list of names from the data like
  names_lst = ["Drs. Losi Walker", ...]

Hint: access the elements of the data and create a formatted string
```
names_lst = [ f"{dta.values[0,0]}" +
              f"{dta.values[0,1]}" + ... ]
```

EXERCISE

Q2. Download the following JSON data file
dropgalaxy.in/qscjjpk629es
and import it and do the following tasks with data:
- slice a section from the data with rows 2,5 & 6 and columns of Name and Dept
- display the data
- in the `ID` column, replace the values with 101 102 103 104 105 106 107 108

Hint: You can extract the values as an array and broadcast it with 100 and then replace or delete that and add it

- display the data
- remove the `StartDate` column
- display the data
- create a DataFrame of Names and Salary like below

	Name	Salary
0	Rick	623.30
1	Dan	515.20
2	Michelle	611.00
3	Ryan	729.00
4	Gary	843.25
5	Nina	578.00
6	Simon	632.80
7	Guru	722.50

Q3. Download the following XLSX data file
dropgalaxy.in/mk8u74zg304x
and clean the data accordingly

09 PYTHON DATABASES

- Databases
- Relational Databases

09 PYTHON DATABASES

Databases

A database is a collection of information that is organized so that it can be easily accessed, managed and updated.

Relational Databases

We can connect to relational databases for analysing data using the pandas library as well as another additional library for implementing database connectivity. This package is named as sqlalchemy which provides full SQL language functionality to be used in python.

We will use **Sqlite3** as our relational database as it is very light weight and easy to use. We will create the relational table by using the to_sql function from a dataframe already created by reading a csv file. Then we use the read_sql_query function from pandas to execute and capture the results from various SQL queries.

SQL is a domain-specific language used in programming and designed for managing data

61 PYTHON DATABASES

```
In [7]: from sqlalchemy import create_engine
        import pandas as pan
        dt = pan.read_csv('csv_data.csv')
        #Create database engine
        eng = create_engine('sqlite:///:memory:')
        # Store the dataframe as a table
        dt.to_sql('data_table', eng)
        #Query
        qri = pan.read_sql_query('SELECT * FROM data_table', eng)
        qri
```

Out[7]:

	index	id	name	price	sales	brand
0	0	101	biscuits	5.00	227	HomeFoods
1	1	102	cookies	7.25	158	TBakery
2	2	103	cake	12.00	50	TBakery
3	3	104	whey_supplement	34.90	24	MusleUp
4	4	105	protein_bars	4.90	85	MusleUp
5	5	106	potato_chips	1.75	121	HomeFoods

We created a DataFrame with CSV data then, we created a database engine create_engine function and next we stored our dataframe in the database with to_sql function of pandas library as data_table

We also created a query in which, we used read_sql_query function to get our data, note that as arguments we passed, 'SELECT * FROM data_table' [data] and eng [engine]

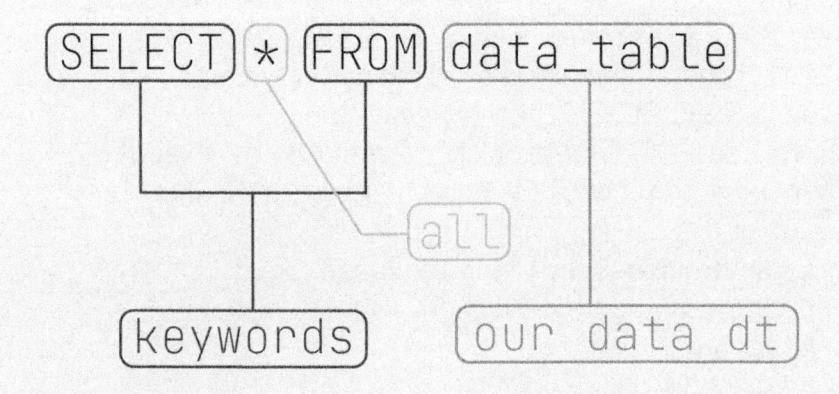

(SELECT) * (FROM) (data_table)
         |
        all
keywords   our data dt

PYTHON DATABASES

We can import selected data

```
In [11]: qri = pan.read_sql_query(
            'SELECT Name,Price FROM data_table',eng
                                )
         qri

Out[11]:
            name          price
         0  biscuits      5.00
         1  cookies       7.25
         2  cake          12.00
         3  whey_supplement  34.90
         4  protein_bars  4.90
         5  potato_chips  1.75
```

or we can import data by groups

```
In [12]: qri = pan.read_sql_query(
            'SELECT Brand,sum(sales) FROM data_table group by Brand'
            ,eng
                                )
         qri

Out[12]:
            brand      sum(sales)
         0  HomeFoods  348
         1  MusleUp    109
         2  TBakery    208
```

In the above code, extracted a grouped data on the basis of brand with data of the brand and its product's sales, we do used the sum function to sump up the total sales of the products from that brand

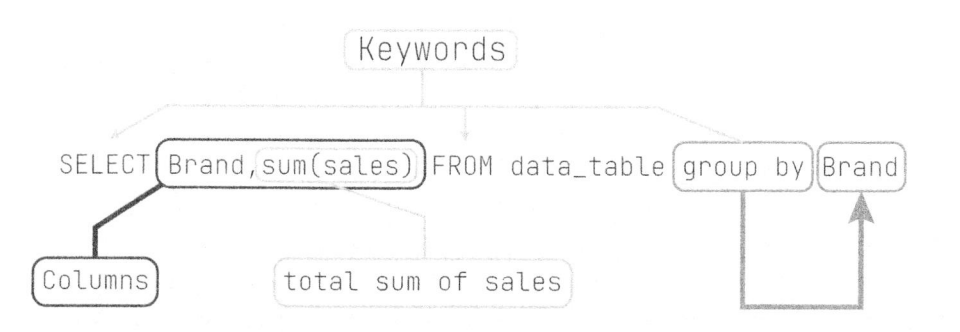

Keywords

SELECT Brand,sum(sales) FROM data_table group by Brand

Columns — total sum of sales

PYTHON DATABASES

Let's say we want to update the database, which we can do that using the `sql.execute` function from `pandas.io` module

```
In [5]: from pandas.io import sql
        sql.execute('INSERT INTO data_table VALUES(?,?,?,?,?,?)'
                    ,eng, params = ['id',107,'gum',0.20,188,'HomeFoods'])
        qri = pan.read_sql_query('SELECT * FROM data_table', eng)
        qri
```

Out[5]:

	index	id	name	price	sales	brand
0	0	101	biscuits	5.00	227	HomeFoods
1	1	102	cookies	7.25	158	TBakery
2	2	103	cake	12.00	50	TBakery
3	3	104	whey_supplement	34.90	24	MusleUp
4	4	105	protein_bars	4.90	85	MusleUp
5	5	106	potato_chips	1.75	121	HomeFoods
6	id	107	gum	0.20	188	HomeFoods

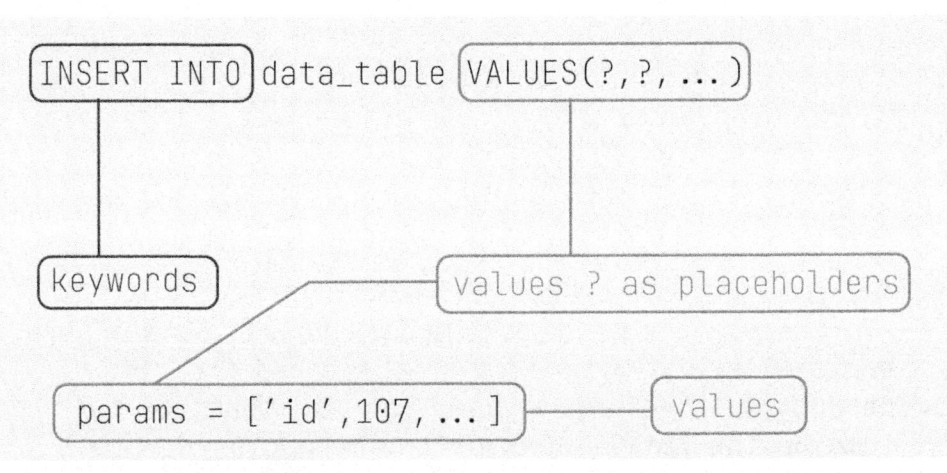

```
INSERT INTO data_table VALUES(?,?, ...)
```
- `INSERT INTO` → keywords
- `VALUES(?,?, ...)` → values ? as placeholders
- `params = ['id',107, ... ]` → values

First of we imported `sql` from the `pandas.io` module and used it to call the `execute` function. In the `execute` function, we specified that we want to insert values in `data_table` using keywords through the `Values(?,?,?,?,?,?)` where, ? are placeholders whose values are defined in the `params` parameter.
Then, we create a query to show our `data_table` with the updated values

PYTHON DATABASES

Like data modification we can also data values using the `execute` function

```
In [5]: from pandas.io import sql
        sql.execute('Delete from data_table where name = (?)',
                    eng, params = [("whey_supplement")])
        qri = pan.read_sql_query('SELECT * FROM data_table', eng)
        qri
Out[5]:
```

	index	id	name	price	sales	brand
0	0	101	biscuits	5.00	227	HomeFoods
1	1	102	cookies	7.25	158	TBakery
2	2	103	cake	12.00	50	TBakery
3	4	105	protein_bars	4.90	85	MusleUp
4	5	106	potato_chips	1.75	121	HomeFoods

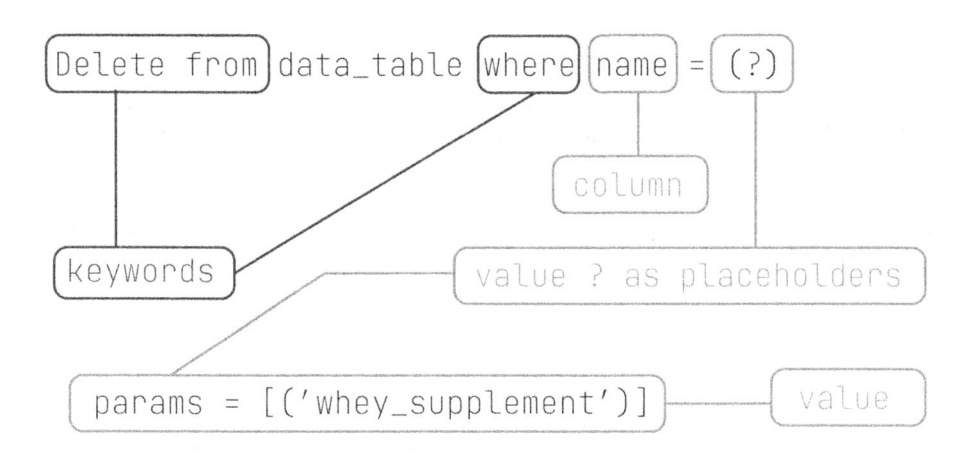

In the `execute` function, we specified that we want to delete a row through the keywords [Delete, from, where] with the (?)[placeholder] value of the column `name` i.e. defined in the `params` parameter ['whey_sepplement']

The whole row with value 'whey_supplement' in the `name` column is removed. Then we create a query to import all the data from `data_table` and display it through the `qri` variable.

Key Points

- A database is a organized data container that can be accessed very eaisly
- Relational databases are not the fastest but best for beginners to learn about databases
- SQL is one of a database that has relational database managing system
- We can create a database using `create_engine` function and store our data using `to_sql` function
- We can create query using the `read_sql_query` function
- We can add, edit or delete data in the SQL database using the `execute` function with keywords like, SELECT, Delete, FROM, Where, Values, etc.

EXERCISE

Q. Create a SQL database and store a csv data[used in previous exercise] in it and do the following tasks:
- create a query to show the rows with TBakery in its Brand column
- add two products with the following attributes
  107   soda   1.25   139   HomeFoods
  108   pie   10.0   57   TBakery
- create a query to show the full data
- delete all the products from TBakery column

10 DATA WRANGLING & AGGREGATION

- Concatenating Data
- Grouping Data
- Applying aggregates on DataFrame

10 DATA WRANGLING AND AGGREGATION

Concatenating Data

Data wrangling involves processing the data in various formats like - merging, grouping, concatenating etc. for the purpose of analysing or getting them ready to be used with another set of data. Python has built-in features to apply these wrangling methods to various data sets to achieve the analytical goal.

We can merge data using the pandas `concat` function

```
In [7]: import pandas as pan
        df1 = pan.DataFrame({
                'id':[101,102,103],
                'Name': ['Biscuits', 'Cookies', 'Cake'],
                'Sales':['227','158','34']})
        df2 = pan.DataFrame(
                {'id':[104,105],
                'Name': ['Pie', 'Bread'],
                'Sales':['26','312']})

        df = pan.concat([ df1, df2])
        df
```

Out[7]:

	id	Name	Sales
0	101	Biscuits	227
1	102	Cookies	158
2	103	Cake	34
0	104	Pie	26
1	105	Bread	312

The `df` data frame is a merged data frame of `df1` and `df2` data frame. We can use `concat` or concatenate function to merge 2 or more data frames.
Note that the indexing is left as it was in the `df1` and `df2` data frame, we can add our own or neglect them

We can pass `True` in the `ignore_index` parameter of the `concat` function

```
In [8]: import pandas as pan
        df1 = pan.DataFrame({
                'id':[101,102,103],
                'Name': ['Biscuits', 'Cookies', 'Cake'],
                'Sales':['227','158','34']})
        df2 = pan.DataFrame(
                {'id':[104,105],
                'Name': ['Pie', 'Bread'],
                'Sales':['26','312']})

        df = pan.concat([ df1, df2], ignore_index = True)
        df

Out[8]:
           id    Name   Sales
        0  101   Biscuits  227
        1  102   Cookies   158
        2  103   Cake      34
        3  104   Pie       26
        4  105   Bread     312
```

We can group data according to similar column items like,

```
In [13]: import pandas as pan
         df = pan.DataFrame({'Team': ['Jackals', 'Jackals', 'Devils', 'Devils', 'Kings',
                'kings', 'Kings', 'Kings', 'Jackals', 'Royals', 'Royals', 'Jackals'],
                'Rank': [1, 2, 2, 3, 3,4 ,1 ,1,2 , 4,1,2],
                'Year': [2019,2018,2019,2018,2019,2018,2016,2017,2016,2019,2018,2017],
                'Points':[876,789,863,673,741,812,756,788,694,701,804,690]})

         dfg = df.groupby('Year')
         dfg.get_group(2018)

Out[13]:
            Team     Rank  Year  Points
         1  Jackals   2    2018   789
         3  Devils    3    2018   673
         5  kings     4    2018   812
         10 Royals    1    2018   804
```

Similarly, we can get data of year 2016, 2017 or 2019

67 DATA AGGREGATION

Applying aggregates on DataFrames

Data aggregation is any process whereby data is gathered and expressed in a summary form. Let's aggregate a Data Frame using the `rolling` function

```
In [16]: import pandas as pan
         import numpy as npy
         ar = npy.array([[1,2,3,4],[6,7,8,9]])
         df = pan.DataFrame((ar),columns = ['C1', 'C2', 'C3', 'C4'])

         ag = df.rolling(window=3,min_periods=1)
         ag

Out[16]: Rolling [window=3,min_periods=1,center=False,axis=0]
```

We can aggregate whole DataFrame

```
In [17]: import pandas as pan
         import numpy as npy
         ar = npy.array([[1,2,3,4],[6,7,8,9]])
         df = pan.DataFrame((ar),columns = ['C1', 'C2', 'C3', 'C4'])

         ag = df.rolling(window=3,min_periods=1)
         ag.aggregate(npy.sum)
```

Out[17]:

	C1	C2	C3	C4
0	1.0	2.0	3.0	4.0
1	7.0	9.0	11.0	13.0

We can aggregate a single column of DataFrame

```
In [21]: import pandas as pan
         import numpy as npy
         ar = npy.array([[1,2,3,4],[6,7,8,9]])
         df = pan.DataFrame((ar),columns = ['C1', 'C2', 'C3', 'C4'])

         ag = df.rolling(window=3,min_periods=1)
         ag['C3'].aggregate(npy.sum)

Out[21]: 0     3.0
         1    11.0
         Name: C3, dtype: float64
```

DATA AGGREGATION

We can aggregate several columns of DataFrame

```
In [22]: import pandas as pan
         import numpy as npy
         ar = npy.array([[1,2,3,4],[6,7,8,9]])
         df = pan.DataFrame((ar),columns = ['C1', 'C2', 'C3', 'C4'])

         ag = df.rolling(window=3,min_periods=1)
         ag['C1','C4'].aggregate(npy.sum)
Out[22]:
```

	C1	C4
0	1.0	4.0
1	7.0	13.0

Key Points

- We can concatenate 2 or more data frames using the concat function
- We can aggregate Data Frames using the rolling function
- We can aggregate the whole data frame using the <data_frame>.aggregate(npy.sum) syntax
- We can aggregate the 1 or more columns in a data frame using the <data_frame>[<columns>].aggregate(npy.sum) syntax

EXERCISE

Q1. Create a 4 data frames with ndarrays. Merge all the data frames into one using proper functions.

Q2. Create a aggregation of the data frame[merged] created above and print it with
window = 2 and min_periods = 1

Q3. Create a aggregation of the even numbered columns of the above data frame adn print it with the default settings.

Q4. What will be the output of the following code cells:

```
In [ ]: import pandas as pan
        import numpy as npy
        ar = npy.array([[4,0,9,1,7],[1,5,3,6,0]])
        ar += 100
        df = pan.DataFrame((ar),columns = ['C1', 'C2', 'C3', 'C4','C5'])

        ag = df.rolling(window = 1, min_periods = 1)
        ag["C2"].aggregate(npy.sum)
```

```
In [ ]: import pandas as pan
        import numpy as npy
        ar = npy.array([[4,0,9,1,7],[1,5,3,6,0]])
        ar += 100
        df = pan.DataFrame((ar),columns = ['C1', 'C2', 'C3', 'C4','C5'])

        ag = df.rolling(window=3,min_periods=1)
        ag['C1','C3','C5'].aggregate(npy.sum)
```

Try to find out the output without running the code, then check your answer with the actual output of the above code

11 READING HTML PAGES

- Beautiful Soup Package
- Reading HTML content
- Working with tag

11 READING HTML PAGES

Beautifulsoup package

Using library known as Beautifulsoup, we can search for the values of html tags and get specific data like title of the page and the list of headers in the page. To use it, we need to istall it through the anaconda prompt with the below code
`conda install beautifulsoup4`

```
Anaconda Prompt (anaconda3)

(base) C:\Users\Rahul>conda install beautifulsoup4
```

Let's import the BeautifulSoup and codecs module. You can use any website you want to extract data from or to keep things easy use the sample data http://bit.ly/sample_html

```
In [11]: import codecs
         from bs4 import BeautifulSoup
         dt = codecs.open('web_file.html','r','utf-8')
         html_data = dt.read()

         # Parse the html file
         s = BeautifulSoup(html_data, 'html.parser')

         # Format the parsed html file
         html = s.prettify()
         html

Out[11]: '<!DOCTYPE html>\n<html>\n <head>\n  <title>\n   Python Data Science\n  </title>\n </head>\n <body>\n  <h1>\n   Data Science\n  </h1>\n  <p>\n ... </html>
```

We used the codecs module's open function to read the import the html file and use it's data. The data in html file is stored in html_data which we pass to the BeautifulSoup for parsing. If we print the parsed data as it is, the data will look ugly that's why we used the prettify function to clean the data and then printed it. Though, you may not understand the HTML code if you're not familiar with it

Reading HTML content

We can extract the html content using html tags like, <title>,<p>,<h1>,etc. Let's extract the tittle of the html page using `title` function

```
In [13]:  import codecs
          from bs4 import BeautifulSoup
          dt = codecs.open('web_file.html','r','utf-8')
          html_data = dt.read()

          s = BeautifulSoup(html_data, 'html.parser')

          print (s.title)
          print(s.title.string)

          <title>Python Data Science</title>
          Python Data Science
```

We can read the whole html file using the `for` loop and `find_all` function

```
In [23]:  import codecs
          from bs4 import BeautifulSoup
          dt = codecs.open('web_file.html','r','utf-8')
          html_data = dt.read()
          s = BeautifulSoup(html_data, 'html.parser')

          for web in s.find_all():
              print(web.string)

          None
          None
          Python Data Science
          None
          Data Science
          Data Science includes data processing, cleaning
```

The `None` represents no value, our html file is small that's why we only see little content, yours may differ according to which html file you chose to work with.

You can also use `urllib.urlopen` function to import a webpage directly

12 DATA SPECIFICATION

- Working with unstructured data
- Word Tokenization
- Stemming and Lemmatization

12 DATA SPECIFICATION

Working with Unstructured data

Until now we worked with data files like CSV, JSON and XLSX which have structured data. But sometimes we get data where the lines are not fixed, or they are just HTML, image or pdf files. Such data is known as unstructured data. For example, a TXT file is just a plain text file. We will try to organize a plain TXT file. You may get the sample file here
http://bit.ly/smpl_txt

```
In [35]: txt = 'text_data.txt'
         with open(txt) as t:
                 # Read each line
                 ln = t.readline()
                 lncnt = 1
                 while ln:
                     print(f"Line {lncnt}: {ln.strip()}")
                     ln = t.readline()
                     lncnt += 1

         Line 1: Biscuits Sales = 227
         Line 2: Cookies Sales = 158
         Line 3: Cakes Sales = 34
         Line 4: Pie Sales = 36
         Line 5: Bread Sales = 121
```

There's a function called `counter` in `collections` that counts the number of words used in a data like,

```
In [36]: from collections import Counter
         with open(r'text_data.txt') as t:
                 p = Counter(t.read().split())
                 print(p)

         Counter({'Sales':  6, '=': 5, 'Biscuits': 1, '227': 1,
         'Cookies': 1, '158': 1, 'Cakes': 1, '34': 1, 'Pie':
         1, '36': 1, 'Bread': 1, '121': 1})
```

Note the use of `with` keyword, which is a very efficient way to work with text files, it opens the file and closes it when it's not needed which saves memory while using large data files

Word Tokenization

Word tokenization is the process of splitting a large sample of text into words. This is a requirement in natural language processing tasks where each word needs to be captured and subjected to further analysis like classifying and counting them for a particular sentiment etc. The Natural Language Tool kit(NLTK) is a library used to achieve this. Install NLTK with anaconda prompt

```
Anaconda Prompt (anaconda3)

(base) C:\Users\Rahul>conda install -c anaconda nltk
```

Use any story or paragraph as data or download the sample TXT file http://bit.ly/nltk_txt_dt
import nltk and use the word_tokenize function

```
In [45]: import nltk
         nltk.download('punkt')
         txt = "Python  is an interpreted, high-level and gene
         nltk_tokens = nltk.word_tokenize(txt)

         nltk_tokens

Out[45]: ['Python',
          'is',
          'an',
          'interpreted',
          ',',
          'high-level',
          'and',
          'general-purpose',
          'programming',
          'language',
          '.',
          'Created',
          'by',
          'Guido',
          'van',
          'Rossum',
          'and',
          'first',
          'released',
          'in'
```

Note the use of `ntlk.download('punkt')` to avoid errors, you may or may not use it. We used `word_tokenize` function to tokenize the text. The output consists of all the words in each line

Like words, we can get the sentence[separated by .] separated in each line using `sent_tokenize` function

```
In [47]: import nltk
         txt = "Python is a beginner friendly language. Pytho
         nltk_tokens = nltk.sent_tokenize(txt)

         nltk_tokens

Out[47]: ['Python is a beginner friendly language.',
          'Python is an OOP language.',
          'Python is easy to learn.']
```

Stemming and Lemmatization

In the areas of Natural Language Processing we come across situation where two or more words have a common root. For example, the three words - agreed, agreeing and agreeable have the same root word agree. A search involving any of these words should treat them as the same word which is the root word. So it becomes essential to link all the words into their root word. The NLTK library has methods to do this linking and give the output showing the root word.

To do that we need import `PorterStemmer` from `nltk.stem.porter`. We need to create a stemmer using `PortStemmer()` function and tokenize the data. In
"Actual: %s   Stem: %s"   %(w,ps.stem(w))
we pass the word in the first %s through the %(w, ...) and the stem in the second %s similarly using stem function. Note the use of C programming

DATA SPECIFICATION

```
In [2]: import nltk
        from nltk.stem.porter import PorterStemmer
        ps = PorterStemmer()
        dt = "It originated from the idea that there are reac
        # Tokenization
        nltk_tokens = nltk.word_tokenize(dt)
        # Stemming
        for w in nltk_tokens:
                print("Actual: %s  Stem: %s"  % (w,ps.stem(w))

        Actual: It      Stem: It
        Actual: originated  Stem: origin
        Actual: from    Stem: from
        Actual: the     Stem: the
        Actual: idea    Stem: idea
        Actual: that    Stem: that
        Actual: there   Stem: there
        Actual: are     Stem: are
        Actual: readers Stem: reader
        Actual: who     Stem: who
        Actual: prefer  Stem: prefer
        Actual: learning  Stem: learn
        Actual: new     Stem: new
        Actual: skills  Stem: skill
```

Lemmatization is similar to stemming but it brings context to the words.So it goes a steps further by linking words with similar meaning to one word. For example if a paragraph has words like cake, bread and cookies, then it will link all of them to bakery. We will WordNet database for this purpose

Import `WordNetLemmatizer` from `nltk.stem` and tokenize the data as done previously. Create the `WordNetLemmatizer()` and use the `lemmatizer` function

You need to download WordNet using

`nltk.download('wordnet')`

command in your Jupyter Notebook after the import statement if you want to avoid errors, it will download it automatically which may take few few seconds.

```
In [8]: import nltk
        from nltk.stem import WordNetLemmatizer

        dt = "It originated from the idea that there are readers who p
        nltk_tokens = nltk.word_tokenize(dt)
        lem = WordNetLemmatizer()

        for w in nltk_tokens:
            print("Actual: %s  Lemma: %s" % (w,lem.lemmatize(w)))

        Actual: It  Lemma: It
        Actual: originated  Lemma: originated
        Actual: from  Lemma: from
        Actual: the  Lemma: the
        Actual: idea  Lemma: idea
        Actual: that  Lemma: that
        Actual: there  Lemma: there
        Actual: are  Lemma: are
        Actual: readers  Lemma: reader
        Actual: who  Lemma: who
        Actual: prefer  Lemma: prefer
        Actual: learning  Lemma: learning
        Actual: new  Lemma: new
        Actual: skills  Lemma: skill
```

Key Points

- We may get to work with structured or unstructured data
- Using the `with` keyword we can save a lot of memory by limiting the storage period of the data file
- The Natural Language Tool Kit [NLTK] helps us to tokenize, stem or lemmatize our data
- We can tokenize data using the `word_tokenize` function by each word or tokenize data using the `sent_tokenize` function by each sentence
- We can stem data using the `PorterSummer()` and `stem` function
- We can lemmatize data using the WordNet database and `lemmatize` function

13 DATA VISUALIZATION

- Pandas, Numpy & Matplotlib
- Plotting a Chart
- Editing labels and colors
- Adding Annotions
- Adding Legends
- Box Plots
- Plotting Heat Maps
- Scatter Plots
- Plotting Bubble Charts
- Plotting 3D Charts
- Time Series
- Plotting graphs
- Sparse graphs

13 DATA VISUALIZATION

Pandas, NumPy & MatPlotLib

Python has excellent libraries for data visualization. A combination of Pandas, numpy and matplotlib can help in creating in nearly all types of visualizations charts.

Plotting a chart

We use `numpy` library to create the required numbers to be mapped for creating the chart and the `pyplot` module of `matplotlib` to draws the actual chart

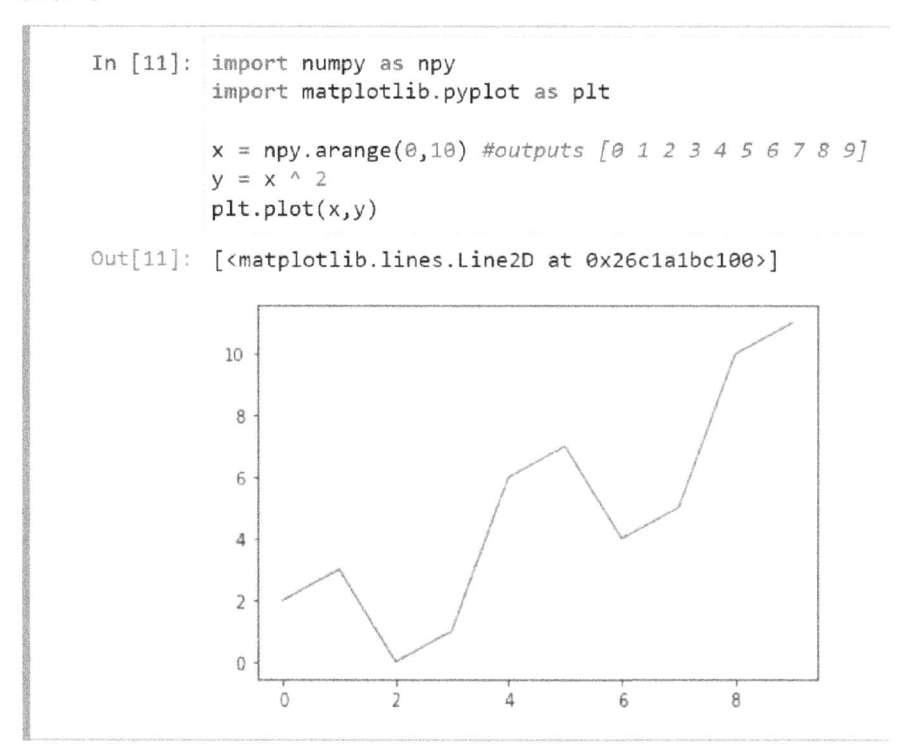

```
In [11]: import numpy as npy
         import matplotlib.pyplot as plt

         x = npy.arange(0,10) #outputs [0 1 2 3 4 5 6 7 8 9]
         y = x ^ 2
         plt.plot(x,y)

Out[11]: [<matplotlib.lines.Line2D at 0x26c1a1bc100>]
```

The `arange(0,10)` function creates a ndarray of numbers from 0 to 10 [excluding 10] and the `plot` function plots a simple chart of the data we provided

Editing labels and colors

As we already know matplotlib uses MATLAB symbols as formatted strings to customize the colors [refer to page 32] and how to add labels to the plots

```
In [15]: import numpy as npy
         import matplotlib.pyplot as plt
         x = npy.arange(0,10)
         y = x ^ 2
         # Editing Labels
         plt.title("Matplotlib")
         plt.xlabel("X_Axis")
         plt.ylabel("Y_Axis")
         # Editing line style and color
         plt.plot(x,y,'c')
         plt.plot(x,y,'*')
```

Out[15]: [<matplotlib.lines.Line2D at 0x26c1a312130>]

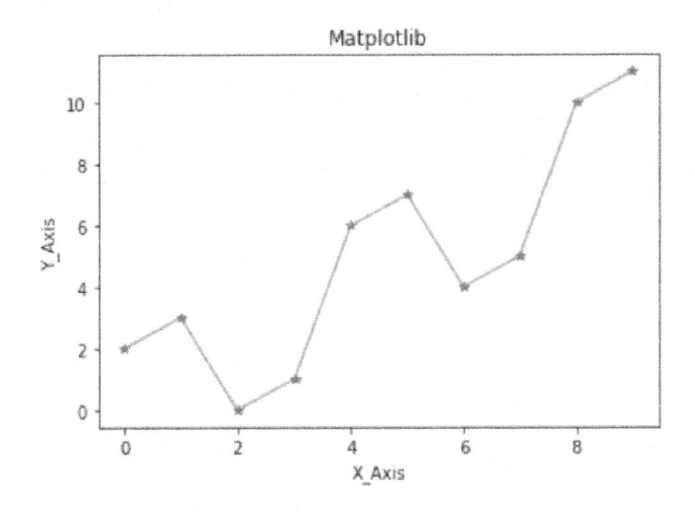

We added a title for the plot Matplolib using the `title` function, X axis and Y axis labels using `xlabel` and `ylabel` functions respectfully.

The 'c' represents cyan which is the color of the line with '*' as symbol for stars

Note that we didn't passed these values in any parameter because they are treated as formatted strings `matplotlib.pyplot.plot` still interprets it as positional argument

Saving the plot

If we want to save the visual, we can use the savefig function

```
In [15]: import numpy as npy
         import matplotlib.pyplot as plt
         x = npy.arange(0,10)
         y = x ^ 2
         # Editing labels
         plt.title("Matplotlib")
         plt.xlabel("X_Axis")
         plt.ylabel("Y_Axis")
         # Editing line style and color
         plt.plot(x,y,'c')
         plt.plot(x,y,'*')

         plt.savefig('data_visual', format = 'png')
```

The file is saved in the directory where your Jupyter Notebook is hosted[refer to page 53]. You can choose any file format like png, svg, pdf, jpg, etc.

Adding annotations

The charts created in python can have further styling by using some appropriate methods from the libraries used for charting. In this lesson we will see the implementation of Annotation, legends and chart background. We will continue to use the plot we created previously and modify it to add these styles to the chart.

Many times, we need to annotate the chart by highlighting the specific locations of the chart. We will highlight the sharp change in values in the chart at those points using annotations

To annotate use the annotate function, pass the values of the coordinates you want to annotate along with label for that point in the s parameter of the annotate function

```
In [19]: import numpy as npy
         import matplotlib.pyplot as plt
         x = npy.arange(0,10)
         y = x ^ 2
         plt.plot(x,y)

         plt.annotate( xy = [2,2], s = 'Day10')
         plt.annotate( xy = [4,8], s = 'Day22')

Out[19]: Text(4, 8, 'Day22')
```

Adding legends

If we want to create a chart with multiple lines being plotted. Use of legend represents the meaning associated with each line. In the below chart we have 3 lines with appropriate legends.

```
In [20]: import numpy as np
         from matplotlib import pyplot as plt
         x = np.arange(0,10)
         y = x ^ 2
         z = x ^ 3
         t = x ^ 4
         plt.plot(x,y)
         plt.plot(x,z)
         plt.plot(x,t)
         plt.legend(['Day1', 'Day2','Day3'], loc=4)
```

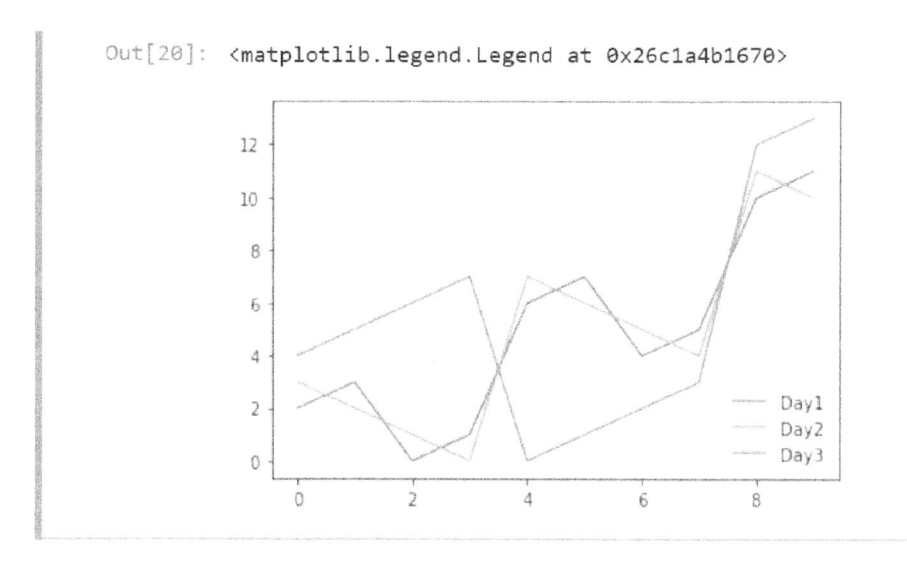

```
Out[20]: <matplotlib.legend.Legend at 0x26c1a4b1670>
```

We used the `plot` function 3 times with different x and y values and also displayed the legend at the bottom left with labels by using the `legend` function

Box Plots

Boxplots are a measure of how well distributed the data in a data set is. It divides the data set into three quartiles. This graph represents the minimum, maximum, median, first quartile and third quartile in the data set. It is also useful in comparing the distribution of data across data sets by drawing boxplots for each of them.

Boxplot can be drawn using `Series.box.plot` function and `DataFrame.box.plot` function or `DataFrame.boxplot` function to visualize the distribution of values within each column. We will use the NumPy's `random.rand` function to generate 2-Dimensional array with 10 1-Dimensional arrays with 5 values in them (`[[1,2,3,4,5],.........]`) the values are floating-point numbers. We will use this ndarray as data for our Data Frame and boxplot it using the `<data_frame>.plot.box()` function

DATA VISUALIZATION

```
In [30]: import pandas as pan
         import numpy as npy
         ar = npy.random.rand(10, 5)
         df = pan.DataFrame(ar, columns=['A','B','C','D','E'])
         df.plot.box()

Out[30]: <matplotlib.axes._subplots.AxesSubplot at 0x26c1c563550>
```

We can show the grid, by passing `True` in the `grid` parameter

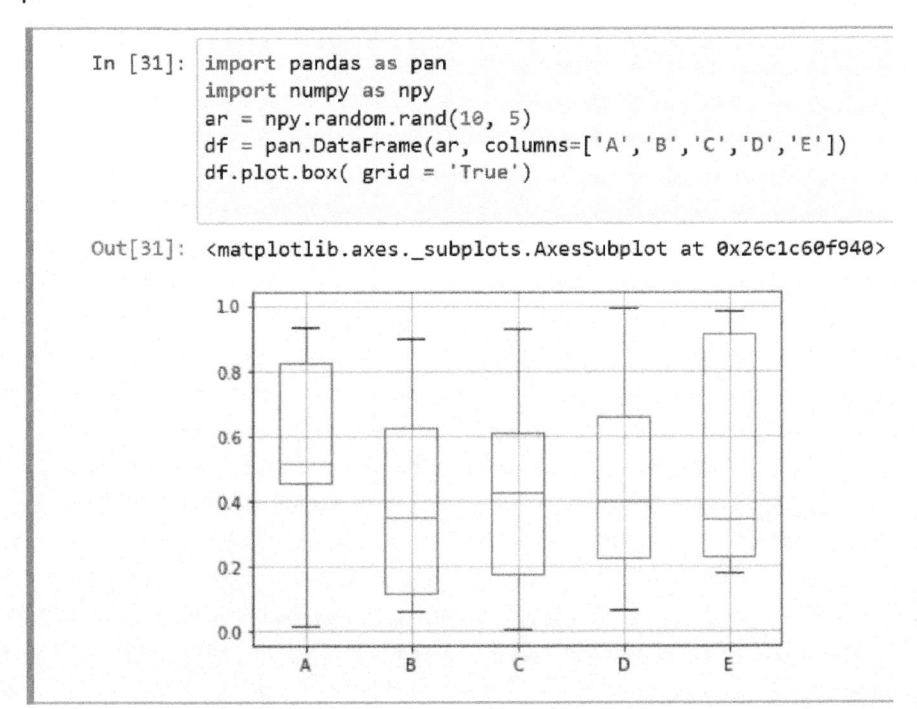

```
In [31]: import pandas as pan
         import numpy as npy
         ar = npy.random.rand(10, 5)
         df = pan.DataFrame(ar, columns=['A','B','C','D','E'])
         df.plot.box( grid = 'True')

Out[31]: <matplotlib.axes._subplots.AxesSubplot at 0x26c1c60f940>
```

Plotting Heat Maps

A heatmap contains values representing various shades of the same colour for each value to be plotted. Usually the darker shades of the chart represent higher values than the lighter shade. For a very different value a completely different colour can also be used.

Create a Data Frame and whose indices and columns will be mapped. We will use the pcolor and show functions to plot the heat map of that Data Frame

```
In [36]: import pandas as pan
         import matplotlib.pyplot as plt

         dt = [{2,3,4,1},{6,3,5,2},
               {6,3,5,4},{3,7,5,4},
               {2,8,1,5}]
         i = ['A', 'B','C','D','E']
         cl = ['C1', 'C2', 'C3','C4']
         df = pan.DataFrame(dt, index = i, columns = cl)

         plt.pcolor(df)
         plt.show()
```

Note the use of {} curly braces insted of box [] to create the data for the heat map. The darker regions like purple in the map reprsents more data and the lighter like yellow represents less data

Scatter plots

Scatterplots show many points plotted in the Cartesian plane. Each point represents the values of two variables. Scatter plot can be created using the `DataFrame.plot.scatter` function and we can determine the size of points in `s` parameter and color in `c` parameter

In [37]:
```python
import pandas as pan
import numpy as npy
dt = npy.random.rand(50, 4)
df = pan.DataFrame(dt, columns=['a', 'b', 'c', 'd'])
df.plot.scatter(x='a', y='b')
```

Out[37]: <matplotlib.axes._subplots.AxesSubplot at 0x26c1c771b80>

In [46]:
```python
df.plot.scatter(x = 'a', y = 'b', s = 3, c = 'a')
```

Out[46]: <matplotlib.axes._subplots.AxesSubplot at 0x26c1ca94730>

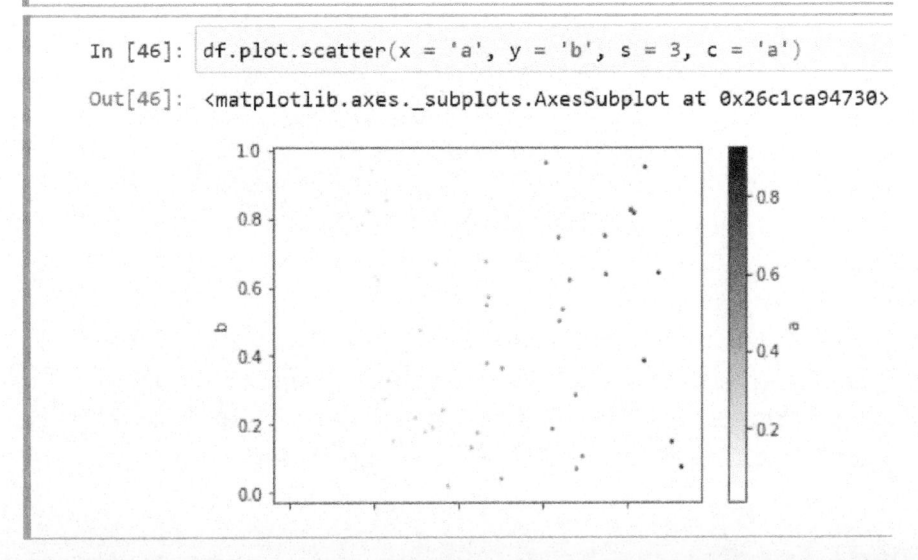

Plotting Bubble charts

Bubble charts display data as a cluster of circles. The required data to create bubble chart needs to have the xy coordinates, size of the bubble and the colour of the bubbles.

```
In [55]: import matplotlib.pyplot as plt
         import numpy as npy

         x = npy.random.rand(50)
         y = npy.random.rand(50)

         sz = npy.random.rand(50)
         clr = npy.random.rand(50)

         # all the values must be same
         # x,y data, size and color values
         plt.scatter(x, y, s = sz*1000, c = clr)

         plt.show()
```

The bubble chart is created with `scatter` function of the `pyplot` module. We passed the x & y value as data, the size of the bubbles[circles] which are increased 1000 times to make them visible clearly and also the color values which are randomly generated that's why the size of the bubble differ from one another, if we passed a single scalar value, it would've been a scatter plot.

Plotting 3D Charts

Python is also capable of creating 3d charts. It involves adding a subplot to an existing two-dimensional plot and assigning the projection parameter as 3d.

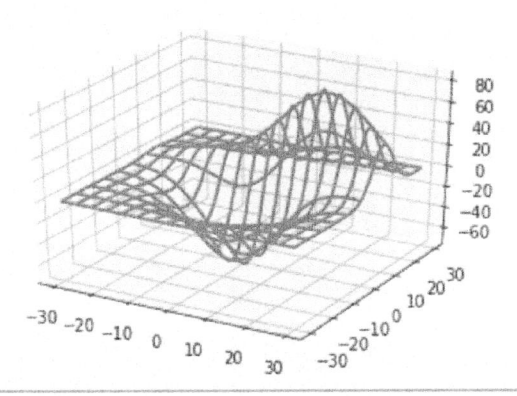

```
In [61]: from mpl_toolkits.mplot3d import axes3d
         import matplotlib.pyplot as plt

         chart = plt.figure()
         chart3d = chart.add_subplot(111, projection='3d')

         # Test Data
         X, Y, Z = axes3d.get_test_data(0.04)

         # Plotting the wireframe.
         chart3d.plot_wireframe(X, Y, Z,
                                color='r',rstride=15, cstride=10)

         plt.show()
```

We imported `axes3d` from `mpl_toolkits.mplot3d`. First of all we create a 3D chart by projecting the `chart` in 3D. We create the data for the three axes with `get_test_data` with 0.04 as the gap between the data, lesser the value more dense the wireframe, more the value less dense the wireframe. Then we use the `plot_wireframe` function with our pre-made data, red as the color, 15 as `rstride`[array row step size] and 10 as `cstride`[array column step size]

Time Series

Time series is a series of data points in which each data point is associated with a timestamp. A simple example is the price of a stock in the stock market at different points of time on a given day.

Download the CSV data file of the prices of a stock in the market at different times
dropgalaxy.in/at0rbl51lfco
also import the `datetime` from `datetime` module

```
In [2]: from datetime import datetime
        import pandas as pan
        import matplotlib.pyplot as plt
        dt = pan.read_csv('stock_market_data.csv')
        df = pan.DataFrame(dt, columns = ['ValueDate', 'Price'])
        # Set the Date as Index
        df['ValueDate'] = pan.to_datetime(df['ValueDate'])
        df.index = df['ValueDate']
        # Delete the local ValueDate column
        del df['ValueDate']

        df.plot()
        plt.show()
```

You may have seen similar graphs in business channels or some other place. We imported the CSV file, in which we created two columns `ValueDate` and `Prices`. Then we changed the values in the `ValueDate` column to `datetime` standards and used them as index as you can see in the graph and then deleted it

Graph Representations

A graph is just a collection of nodes, which have links between them. Graphs can represent nearly anything - social network connections, where each node is a person and is connected to acquaintances; images, where each node is a pixel and is connected to neighbouring pixels; points in a high-dimensional distribution, where each node is connected to its nearest neighbours and practically anything else you can imagine.

The creation of the sparse graph submodule was motivated by several algorithms used in scikit-learn that included:
- Isomap - A manifold learning algorithm, which requires finding the shortest paths in a graph.
- Hierarchical clustering - A clustering algorithm based on a minimum spanning tree.
- Spectral Decomposition - A projection algorithm based on sparse graph laplacians.

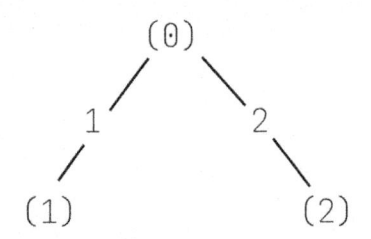

```
        (0)
       /   \
     1/     \2
     /       \
   (1)       (2)
```

This graph has three nodes, where node 0 and 1 are connected by an edge of weight 2, and nodes 0 and 2 are connected by an edge of weight 1. We can construct the dense, masked and sparse representations as shown in the following example, keeping in mind that an undirected graph is represented by a symmetric matrix.

To create it, we need to import csr_matrix from scipy.sparse module. We create a ndarray and use the ma.masked function and csr_matrix function to mask and sparse the data in the ndarray

```
In [6]:  import numpy as np
         from scipy.sparse import csr_matrix

         dns = np.array([ [0, 2, 1],
                          [2, 0, 0],
                          [1, 0, 0] ])

         # masking data
         msk = np.ma.masked_values(dns, 0)

         # sparsing data
         spr = csr_matrix(dns)
         spr

Out[6]:  <3x3 sparse matrix of type '<class 'numpy.intc'>'
             with 4 stored elements in Compressed Sparse Row format>

In [7]:  spr.data

Out[7]:  array([2, 1, 2, 1], dtype=int32)
```

Key Points

- A combination of Pandas, numpy and matplotlib can help in creating in nearly all types of visualizations charts.
- We can plot any data using `matplotlib.pyplot` function
- The title, axis labels, line styles, points shape and colors of a plot can be customized
- We can also add annotations using the `annotate` function and add legends to multi-line graphs using the `legend` function
- We can create boxplots, scatter plots and plot heat maps using pandas data frames
- We can also create 3D maps using `axes3d` function
- We can also use `datetime` in pandas data frames when dealing with dates or time

EXERCISE

Q1. Using the plot function plot a graph of the followig data:

x values = 21, 33, 35, 37, 49, 55
y values = 10, 20, 30, 40, 50, 60

and perform the following tasks:
- title the plot as Sales_Data
- label the x axis as Sales
- label the y_axis as Period
- annote the maximum rise in sales with Max Rise
- add second data in it as:

x values = 12, 19, 24, 33, 45, 58
y values = same as above

also add legend for the upper data as 'Cookies' and the new data as 'Cakes'
- display the data

Q2. Try converting the above data into the followings and check whether they can be or not:
- BoxPlot
- Heat Map
- Scatter Plot
- Bubble graphs

14 MEASURING DATA

- Calculating Mean and Median
- Calculating Mode
- Measuring Variance

14 MEASURING DATA

Calculating Mean and Median

Mean is the Average value of the data which is a division of sum of the values with the number of values and Median is the middle value in distribution when the values are arranged in ascending or descending order. which we can calculate easily using pandas data frames

Create a data frame and use the mean and median functions

```
In [2]: import pandas as pan
        dt = {'Sales':[ 227, 158, 34, 121],
              'Price':[ 5.0, 7.5, 12, 3.5]}
        df = pan.DataFrame(dt)
```

```
In [4]: df.mean()
```
```
Out[4]: Sales    135.0
        Price      7.0
        dtype: float64
```

```
In [5]: df.median()
```
```
Out[5]: Sales    139.50
        Price      6.25
        dtype: float64
```

We get mean and median of each column in the data frame, Sales and Price. Note that if you use df.mean instead of df.mean(), you'll get the result but a bit in disorder

Calculating Mode

Mode is the most commonly occurring value in a distribution. The data we used for calculating Mean and Median cannot be used here because it doesn't have any commonly occuring value

To calculate the mode, we need to use the pandas mode function

```
In [8]: import pandas as pan
        dt = {'Day':pan.Series([ 'D1', 'D2', 'D3', 'D4', 'D5']),
              'Sales':pan.Series([ 127, 133, 96, 133, 117])}
        df = pan.DataFrame(dt)

In [9]: df.mode()
```

Out[9]:

	Day	Sales
0	D1	133.0
1	D2	NaN
2	D3	NaN
3	D4	NaN
4	D5	NaN

We got the Day column as it is because every value in it is unique and got 133[that occured twice] at top with other values as NaN. If use the Sales column only you'll get a more clean output

```
In [11]: import pandas as pan
         dt = {'Day':pan.Series([ 'D1', 'D2', 'D3', 'D4', 'D5']),
               'Sales':pan.Series([ 127, 133, 96, 133, 117])}
         df = pan.DataFrame(dt)
         df
```

Out[11]:

	Day	Sales
0	D1	127
1	D2	133
2	D3	96
3	D4	133
4	D5	117

```
In [10]: df['Sales'].mode()
Out[10]: 0    133
         dtype: int64
```

Measuring Variance

In statistics, variance is a measure of how far a value in a data set lies from the mean value. In other words, it indicates how dispersed the values are. It is measured by using standard deviation.

Standard deviation is square root of variance. variance is the average of squared difference of values in a data set from the mean value. We can use the std() function to calculate it

```
In [13]: import pandas as pan
         dt = {'Sales':[ 127, 133, 96, 133, 117],
               'Price':[ 12,5,11.5,6.5,4]}
         df = pan.DataFrame(dt)
```

```
In [14]: df.std()
Out[14]: Sales    15.530615
         Price     3.718198
         dtype: float64
```

Skewness is used to determine whether the data is symmetric or skewed. If the index is between -1 and 1, then the distribution is symmetric. If the index is no more than -1 then it is skewed to the left and if it is at least 1, then it is skewed to the right.

We can use the skew() function on the above data to find the skewness

```
In [15]: df.skew()
Out[15]: Sales   -1.401047
         Price    0.370593
         dtype: float64
```

The Sales data is skewed to the left [$i \geq 1$] and the Prices data is symmetric [$-1 \leq i \geq 1$]

Note that these are statistical data that is used often a lot that's why they are included in pandas library

Key Points

- We can find the mean, median and mode of data frames using `mean()`, `median()` and `mode()` functions respectively
- We can find the standard deviation of a data frame using `std()` function
- We can find the Skewness of a data frame using the `skew()` function

EXERCISE

Q1. Create a data frame with the following data:

```
ID     s1 s2 s3 s4 s5 s6 s7 s8 s9 s10
Marks  88 52 76 88 93 70 52 86 88 100
```

and perform the following tasks:
- calculate the total marks
- calculate the average marks
- calculate the median of the marks
- calculate how many students got the same marks and how many times

Hint: Perform `mode()` only on that column

- print all the results as follows: [next page]

EXERCISE

	Total Marks	Avg. Marks	Median Mark		Marks	Students
1	<marks>	<marks>	<marks>	0	<marks>	<times>
				1	<marks>	<times>
				2	<marks>	<times>
				3	<marks>	<times>

Q2. Create a data frame with the following data:

```
ID    xc ya xb xe yc yb xf ye xr yn
Sales 14 16 21 32 66 16 34 77 12 16
```

and perform the following tasks:
- calculate the total sales
- calculate the average sales
- calculate the median of the sales
- calculate mode of the sales
- calculate the standard deviation of the sales
- calculate the skewness of the data
- print all the results as done previously

15 DATA DISTRIBUTION

- Normal Distribution
- Binomial Distribution
- Poisson Distribution
- Bernoulli Distribution

15 DATA DISTRIBUTION

Normal Distribution

The normal distribution is a form presenting data by arranging the probability distribution of each value in the data. Most values remain around the mean value making the arrangement symmetric.
We will create a normal distribution curve

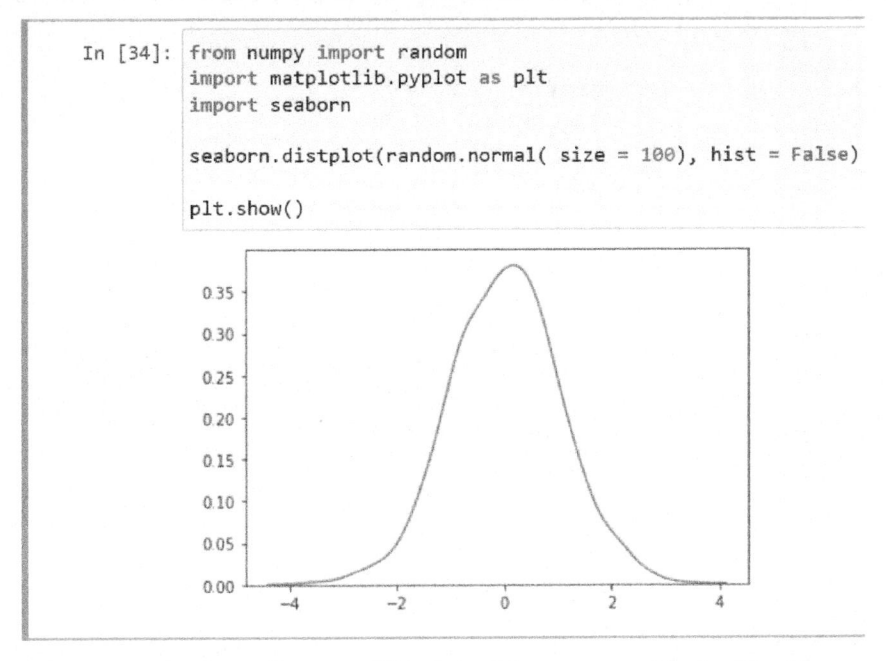

```
In [34]: from numpy import random
         import matplotlib.pyplot as plt
         import seaborn

         seaborn.distplot(random.normal( size = 100), hist = False)

         plt.show()
```

The graph is also called bell-paper distribution due it's shape
We used the `seaborn` module's `distplot` to plot the graph with normal distributed data values from the `random.normal` function

Binomial Distribution

The binomial distribution model deals with finding the probability of success of an event which has only two possible outcomes in a series of experiments. For example, tossing of a coin always gives a head or a tail. The probability of finding exactly 3 heads in tossing a coin repeatedly for 10 times is estimated during the binomial distribution.

We will use the `scipy` packages `binom` module to create the binomial distribution

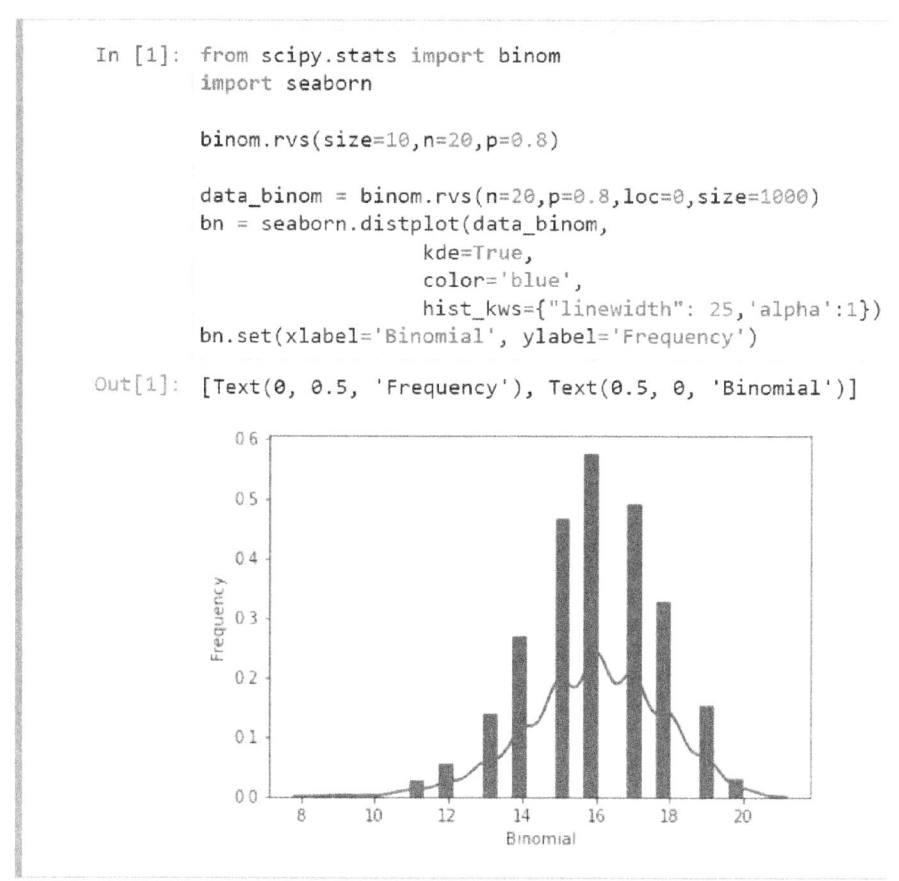

```
In [1]: from scipy.stats import binom
        import seaborn

        binom.rvs(size=10,n=20,p=0.8)

        data_binom = binom.rvs(n=20,p=0.8,loc=0,size=1000)
        bn = seaborn.distplot(data_binom,
                    kde=True,
                    color='blue',
                    hist_kws={"linewidth": 25,'alpha':1})
        bn.set(xlabel='Binomial', ylabel='Frequency')

Out[1]: [Text(0, 0.5, 'Frequency'), Text(0.5, 0, 'Binomial')]
```

Poisson Distribution

A Poisson distribution is a distribution which we willshows the likely number of times that an event will occur within a pre-determined period of time. It is used for independent events which occur at a constant rate within a given interval of time. The Poisson distribution is a discrete function, meaning that the event can only be measured as

occurring or not as occurring, meaning the variable can only be measured in whole numbers.
We will use the poisson module of the scipy package like we did before to create the poisson distribution

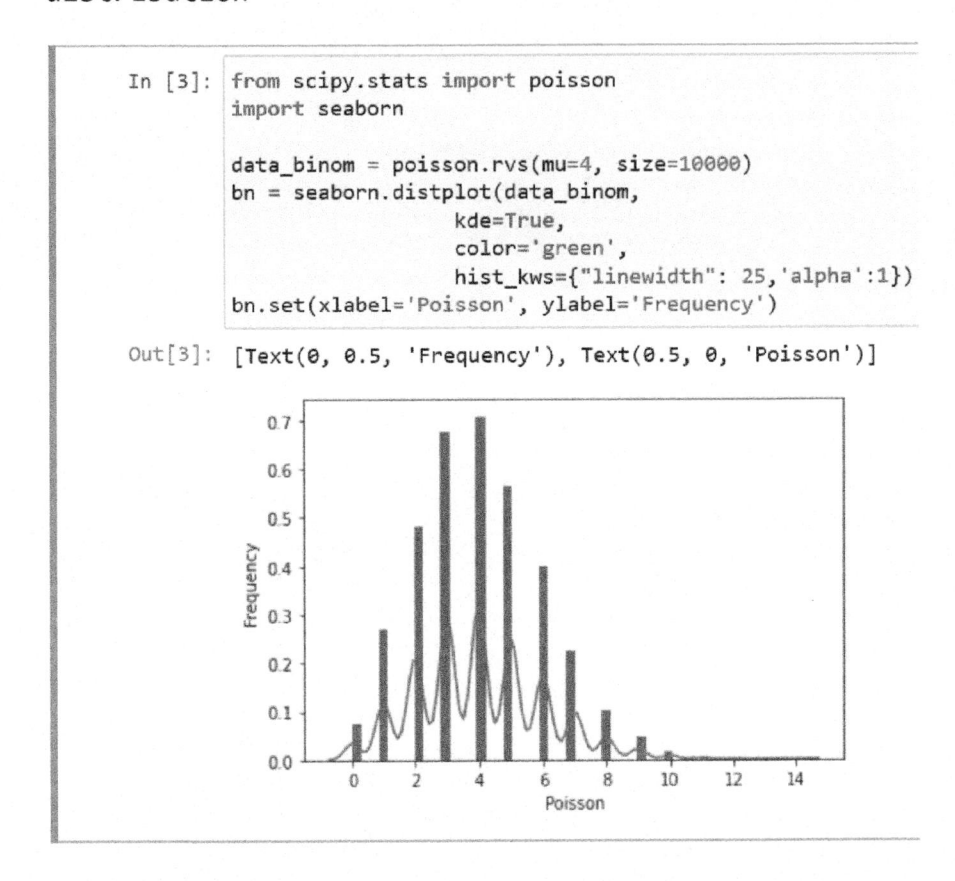

```
In [3]: from scipy.stats import poisson
import seaborn

data_binom = poisson.rvs(mu=4, size=10000)
bn = seaborn.distplot(data_binom,
                kde=True,
                color='green',
                hist_kws={"linewidth": 25,'alpha':1})
bn.set(xlabel='Poisson', ylabel='Frequency')
Out[3]: [Text(0, 0.5, 'Frequency'), Text(0.5, 0, 'Poisson')]
```

Bernoulli Distribution

The Bernoulli distribution is a special case of the Binomial distribution where a single experiment is conducted so that the number of observation is 1. So, the Bernoulli distribution therefore describes events having exactly two outcomes.
We will use the bernoulli module of the scipy package to create the bernoulli distribution of data

DATA DISTRIBUTION

```
In [4]: from scipy.stats import bernoulli
        import seaborn

        data_bern = bernoulli.rvs(size=1000,p=0.6)
        bn = seaborn.distplot(data_bern,
                        kde=True,
                        color='crimson',
                        hist_kws={"linewidth": 25,'alpha':0.5})
        bn.set(xlabel='Bernouli', ylabel='Frequency')

Out[4]: [Text(0, 0.5, 'Frequency'), Text(0.5, 0, 'Bernouli')]
```

Note that I passed 0.5 in the `hist_kws`'s `alpha` parameter to show the histogram graphs at 50% opacity or transparency.

16 DATA TESTS

- P-Value
- Correlations
- Chi-Square Test

16 DATA TESTS

P-Value

The p-value is about the strength of a hypothesis. We build hypothesis based on some statistical model and compare the model's validity using p-value. One way to get the p-value is by using T-tests.

This is a two-sided test for the null hypothesis that the expected value (mean) of a sample of independent observations 'a' is equal to the given population mean, *popmean*.

We will use the scipy package to perform it

```
In [5]: from scipy import stats as sts
        rvs = sts.norm.rvs(loc = 5, scale = 10, size = (50,2))
        sts.ttest_1samp(rvs,5.0)

Out[5]: Ttest_1sampResult(statistic=array([-0.56915379, 0.54310825]),
        pvalue=array([0.57185164, 0.58951749]))
```

Comparing samples

We will use two samples, which can come either from the same or from different distribution, and we want to test whether these samples have the same statistical properties.

```
In [7]: from scipy import stats as sts
        rvs1 = sts.norm.rvs(loc = 5,scale = 10,size = 500)
        rvs2 = sts.norm.rvs(loc = 5,scale = 10,size = 500)
        sts.ttest_ind(rvs1,rvs2)

Out[7]: Ttest_indResult(statistic = 0.21262155812273673,
        pvalue = 0.8316655746236457)
```

ttest_ind - Calculates the T-test for the means of two independent samples of scores. This is a two-sided test for the null hypothesis that two independent samples have identical average (expected) values. This test assumes that the populations have identical variances by default.

You can test the same with a new array of the same length, but with a varied mean. Use a different value in loc and test the same.

Correlations

Correlation refers to some statistical relationships involving dependence between two data sets. Simple examples of dependent phenomena include the correlation between the physical appearance of parents and their offspring, and the correlation between the price for a product and its supplied quantity.

```
In [12]: import matplotlib.pyplot as plt
         import seaborn
         df = seaborn.load_dataset('iris')
         seaborn.pairplot(df, kind="scatter")
         plt.show()
```

We take example of the `iris` data set available in seaborn python library. In it we try to establish the correlation between the length and the width of the sepals and petals of three species of iris flower. Based on the correlation found, a strong model could be created which easily distinguishes one species from another.

The output data visuals:

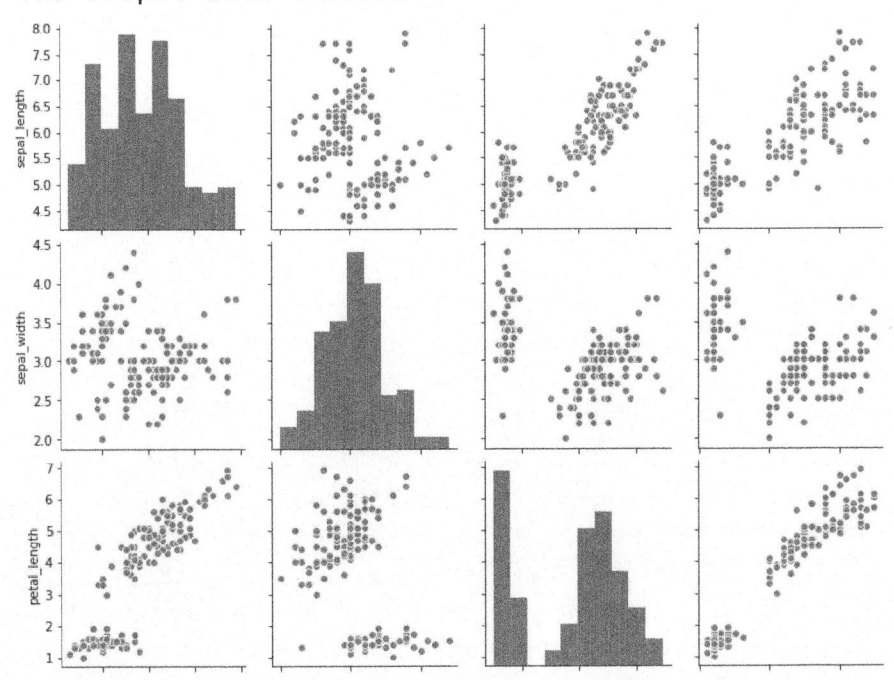

Chi-square test

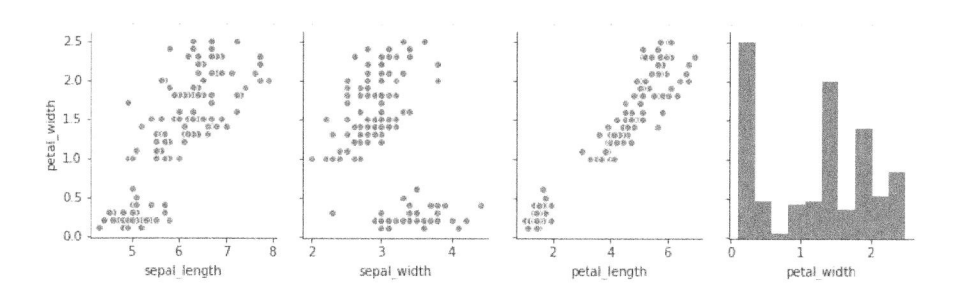

Chi-Square test is a statistical method to determine if two categorical variables have a significant correlation between them. Both those variables should be from same population and they should be categorical like - Yes/No, Male/Female, Red/Green etc. For example, we can build a data set with observations on people's ice-cream buying pattern and try to correlate the gender of a person with the flavour of the ice-cream they prefer.

If a correlation is found we can plan for appropriate stock of flavours by knowing the number of gender of people visiting.

We will use the numpy and scipy libraries along with matplotlib to visualize our data

```
In [13]:  from scipy import stats
          import numpy as npy
          import matplotlib.pyplot as plt

          x = npy.linspace(0, 10, 100)
          fig,ax = plt.subplots(1,1)

          linestyles = [':', '--', '-.', '-']
          deg_of_freedom = [1, 4, 7, 6]
          for df, ls in zip(deg_of_freedom, linestyles):
              ax.plot(x, stats.chi2.pdf(x, df), linestyle=ls)

          plt.xlim(0, 10)
          plt.ylim(0, 0.4)
          plt.xlabel('Value')
          plt.ylabel('Frequency')
          plt.title('Chi-Square Distribution')
          plt.show()
```

109 DATA TESTS

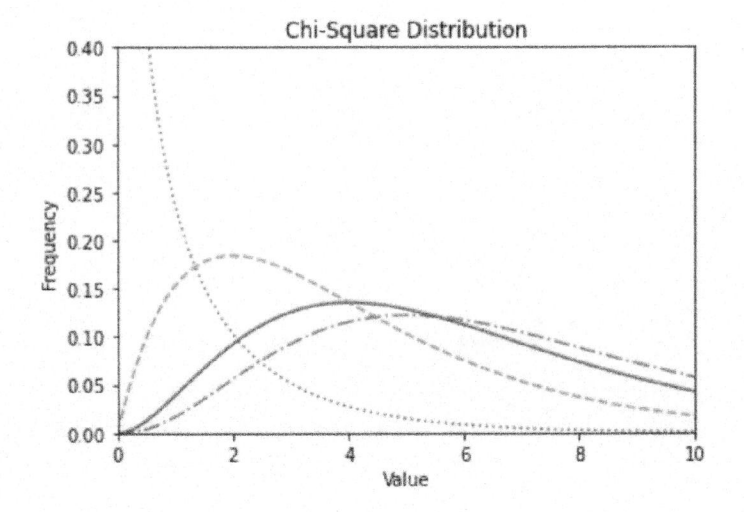

Chi-Square Distribution

17 PROJECT

We will work with a CSV-data file

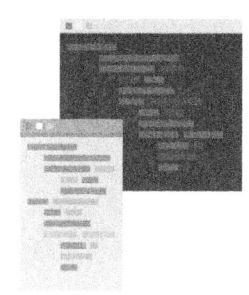

17 DATA SCIENCE PROJECT

CSV data file

We will work with a dataset of the measurements of different trees. Download the file here
http://bit.ly/trees_csv_dt

We will create a report of the data set with the best practices we have learned so far

Importing the CSV data

We will use the pandas `read_csv` function to import our data

```
In [1]: import pandas as pan

        dt = pan.read_csv('trees.csv')
        dt
```

Out[1]:

Index	"Girth (in)"	"Height (ft)"	"Volume(ft^3)"
0	1	8.3	70	10.3
1	2	8.6	65	10.3
2	3	8.8	63	10.2
3	4	10.5	72	16.4
4	5	10.7	81	18.8
5	6	10.8	83	19.7
6	7	11.0	66	15.6
7	8	11.0	75	18.2
8	9	11.1	80	22.6
9	10	11.2	75	19.9
10	11	11.3	79	24.2
11	12	11.4	76	21.0
12	13	11.4	76	21.4
13	14	11.7	69	21.3

The data has 30 rows and 4 columns. It needs a lot of cleaning, which we will do next

Data Cleansing

The data has a extra index column which needs to removed and the others columns needs to be renamed

In [3]:
```
import pandas as pan

dt = pan.read_csv('trees.csv',
                  names = ['Index','Girth',
                           'Height','Volume'])
del dt['Index']
dt
```

Out[3]:

	Girth	Height	Volume
0	"Girth (in)"	"Height (ft)"	"Volume(ft^3)"
1	8.3	70	10.3
2	8.6	65	10.3
3	8.8	63	10.2
4	10.5	72	16.4
5	10.7	81	18.8
6	10.8	83	19.7
7	11.0	66	15.6
8	11.0	75	18.2
9	11.1	80	22.6
10	11.2	75	19.9
11	11.3	79	24.2

We passed the index labels in the names parameter in the read_csv function or while the creation of the data frame from the csv data. We also removed the Index column using the del keyword. But the default column labels are treated as values

We need to remove the first row or the 0 indexed row which is the column labels of the csv data. We also need to change all the values in terms of metre because the girth is in inches, the height is in feet and the volume is in feet cube

We dropped the first row using the `drop` function, and using True in the `inplace` parameter, the data frame starts with 1 as the starting index instead of 0 i.e. everything stays in place as they were before

```
In [4]: import pandas as pan

        dt = pan.read_csv('trees.csv',
                        names = ['Index','Girth',
                                 'Height','Volume'])
        del dt['Index']
        dt.drop(0, inplace = True)

        dt['Girth'] = dt['Girth'].astype(float)
        dt['Height'] = dt['Height'].astype(float)
        dt['Volume'] = dt['Volume'].astype(float)

        dt['Girth'] *= 0.0254
        dt['Height'] *= 0.305
        dt['Volume'] *= 0.0283
        dt
```

Out[4]:

	Girth	Height	Volume
1	0.21082	21.350	0.29149
2	0.21844	19.825	0.29149
3	0.22352	19.215	0.28866
4	0.26670	21.960	0.46412
5	0.27178	24.705	0.53204
6	0.27432	25.315	0.55751

Next, we changed the type of all the data values as `float` using the `astype` function which changes all the values of whole dataframe, column or row. We did so to prevent any errors while multiplying them. After that, we changed them all in terms of metres, the Girth values which were in inches are multiplied with 0.0254[as 1 inch = 0.0254 metre], the height values which were in foot are multiplied with 0.305[as 1 foot = 0.03048 metre] and the volume values which were in cubic foot are multiplied with 0.0283 [as 1 cubic foot = 0.0283 cubic metre]

114 PROJECT

All the values are in terms of metre, but they are not clean, with 5 digits after the decimal point. We need round them off

```
In [5]: import pandas as pan

        dt = pan.read_csv('trees.csv',
                        names = ['Index','Girth',
                                  'Height','Volume'])
        del dt['Index']
        dt.drop(0, inplace = True)

        dt['Girth']  = dt['Girth'].astype(float)
        dt['Height'] = dt['Height'].astype(float)
        dt['Volume'] = dt['Volume'].astype(float)

        dt['Girth']  *= 0.0254
        dt['Height'] *= 0.305
        dt['Volume'] *= 0.0283

        dt.round(1)
Out[5]:
```

	Girth	Height	Volume
1	0.2	21.3	0.3
2	0.2	19.8	0.3
3	0.2	19.2	0.3
4	0.3	22.0	0.5
5	0.3	24.7	0.5

We used the round function and passed 1 as the decimal place after the decimal point. Now, our data looks clean

Data cleansing is done! Now we need to find the max and minimum girth, height and volume. Also we need to find the average, median and mode of girth, height and volume of the tress. After calculating all those we need to print them accordingly on the terminal

Let's move on to the next step i.e. measuring the data. We already know all the methods to measure our data

Measuring data

First of all let's find out all the maximum and minimum values. Note that we will perform each step in a new cell to organize things

```
In [6]:  max_girth = dt['Girth'].max()
         max_height = dt['Height'].max()
         max_vol = dt['Volume'].max()

         min_girth = dt['Girth'].min()
         min_height = dt['Height'].min()
         min_vol = dt['Volume'].min()

         print(max_girth, max_height, max_vol)
         print(min_girth, min_height, min_vol)

         0.52324 26.535 2.1791
         0.21082 19.215 0.28865999999999997
```

The maximum values can be find using the `max` function and the minimum values can be found using the `min` value. The values are not rounded off so let's do it

```
In [7]:  max_girth = (dt['Girth'].round(2)).max()
         max_height = (dt['Height'].round(2)).max()
         max_vol = (dt['Volume'].round(2)).max()

         min_girth = (dt['Girth'].round(2)).min()
         min_height = (dt['Height'].round(2)).min()
         min_vol = (dt['Volume'].round(2)).min()

         print(max_girth, max_height, max_vol)
         print(min_girth, min_height, min_vol)

         0.52 26.54 2.18
         0.21 19.22 0.29
```

Note that we rounded up the values using the round function with 2 decimal places befor finding the maximum or minimum values. Also, the parentheses are important

PROJECT

Now let's find the average, median and mode values of the data

```
In [8]: max_girth = (dt['Girth'].round(2)).max()
        max_height = (dt['Height'].round(2)).max()
        max_vol = (dt['Volume'].round(2)).max()

        min_girth = (dt['Girth'].round(2)).min()
        min_height = (dt['Height'].round(2)).min()
        min_vol = (dt['Volume'].round(2)).min()

        avg_girth = round(dt['Girth'].mean(), 2)
        med_girth = (dt['Girth'].round(2)).median()
        mod_girth = (dt['Girth'].round(2)).mode()

        avg_height = round(dt['Height'].mean(), 2)
        med_height = (dt['Height'].round(2)).median()
        mod_height = (dt['Height'].round(2)).mode()

        avg_vol = round(dt['Volume'].mean(), 2)
        med_vol = (dt['Volume'].round(2)).median()
        mod_vol = (dt['Volume'].round(2)).mode()

        print(avg_girth, med_girth, mod_girth)
        print(avg_height, med_height, mod_height)
        print(avg_vol, med_vol, mod_vol)

        0.34 0.33 0    0.28
        dtype: float64
        23.18 23.18 0    24.4
        dtype: float64
        0.85 0.68 0    0.29
        dtype: float64
```

By using the mean, median and mode functions we calculated the average, median and mode of the data. Note that we rounded off the values first using the round function before calculating the median and mode

While calculating the mean, we didn't used the DataFrame's round function first because the mean function can return a lengthy float and in our case it will that's why, we first calculated the mean and then rounded off the result using the built-in round function to 2 decimal places

Data Visualization

We have calculated all the details we needed for our report now, we need to generate some charts to visualize our data

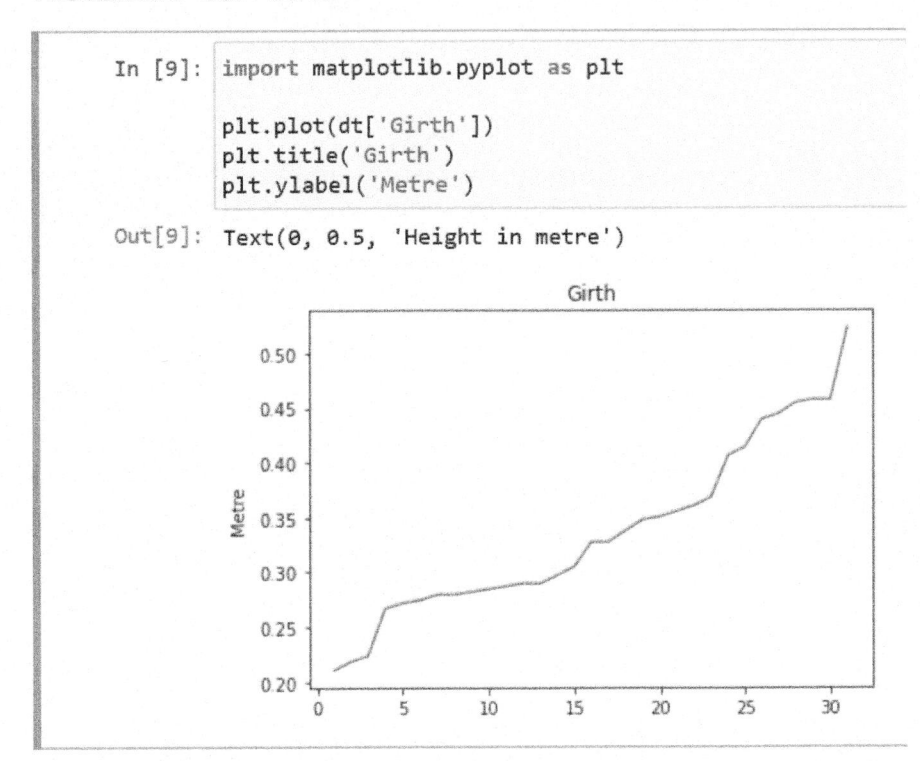

```
In [9]: import matplotlib.pyplot as plt

        plt.plot(dt['Girth'])
        plt.title('Girth')
        plt.ylabel('Metre')

Out[9]: Text(0, 0.5, 'Height in metre')
```

We plotted the Girth data using the data frames Girth column. Note that the title and the Y-axis label are also added

```
In [ ]: plt.plot(dt['Height'])
        plt.title('Height')
        plt.ylabel('Metre')
```

Likewise we will create the plots for the Height and Volume. Note that the plots for Girth, Height and Volume data are create in different cells and you should to, to keep things organized and easy to edit

```
In [10]: plt.plot(dt['Height'])
         plt.title('Height')
         plt.ylabel('Metre')
```

Out[10]: Text(0, 0.5, 'Metre')

```
In [11]: plt.plot(dt['Volume'])
         plt.title('Volume')
         plt.ylabel('Cubic Metre')
```

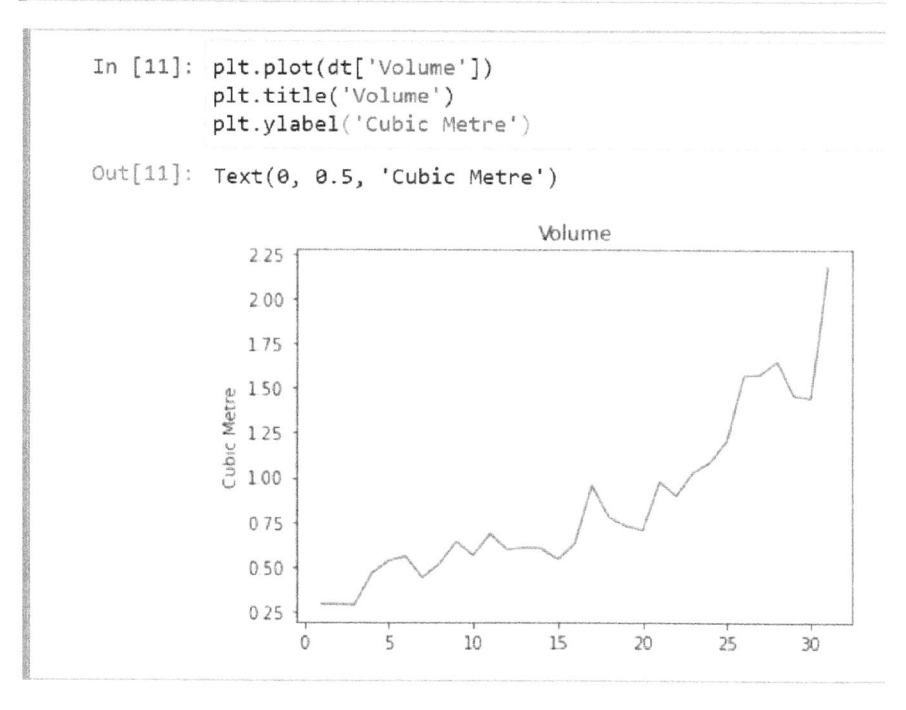

Out[11]: Text(0, 0.5, 'Cubic Metre')

Perfect, now we can generate our report

Report

Now we need to combine all the data and display it, you can also create an pdf or other document file using the output
Here is the full length code and the generated output

```python
In [12]:  # Importing packages and modules we need
          import pandas as pan
          import matplotlib.pyplot as plt

          # Importing data
          dt = pan.read_csv('trees.csv',
                          names = ['Index','Girth',
                                   'Height','Volume'])
          # Cleaning the data
          del dt['Index']
          dt.drop(0, inplace = True)

          dt['Girth'] = dt['Girth'].astype(float)
          dt['Height'] = dt['Height'].astype(float)
          dt['Volume'] = dt['Volume'].astype(float)

          dt['Girth'] *= 0.0254
          dt['Height'] *= 0.305
          dt['Volume'] *= 0.0283

          # Measuring the data
          max_girth = (dt['Girth'].round(2)).max()
          max_height = (dt['Height'].round(2)).max()
          max_vol = (dt['Volume'].round(2)).max()

          min_girth = (dt['Girth'].round(2)).min()
          min_height = (dt['Height'].round(2)).min()
          min_vol = (dt['Volume'].round(2)).min()

          avg_girth = round(dt['Girth'].mean(), 2)
          med_girth = (dt['Girth'].round(2)).median()
          mod_girth = (dt['Girth'].round(2)).mode()

          avg_height = round(dt['Height'].mean(), 2)
          med_height = (dt['Height'].round(2)).median()
          mod_height = (dt['Height'].round(2)).mode()
```

PROJECT

```python
avg_girth = round(dt['Girth'].mean(), 2)
med_girth = (dt['Girth'].round(2)).median()
mod_girth = (dt['Girth'].round(2)).mode()

avg_height = round(dt['Height'].mean(), 2)
med_height = (dt['Height'].round(2)).median()
mod_height = (dt['Height'].round(2)).mode()

avg_vol = round(dt['Volume'].mean(), 2)
med_vol = (dt['Volume'].round(2)).median()
mod_vol = (dt['Volume'].round(2)).mode()

# Creating table of the calculated data
df = pan.DataFrame({'Girth':[max_girth, min_girth,
                            avg_girth, med_girth,
                            mod_girth[0]],
                   'Height':[max_height, min_height,
                            avg_height, med_height,
                            mod_height[0]],
                   'Volume':[max_vol, min_vol,
                            avg_vol, med_vol,
                            mod_vol[0]]},
                  index = ['Maximum', 'Minimum',
                           'Average', 'Median','Mode'])

# Displaying the data
print('Tree measurements data\n')
print(dt.round(1), end = '\n\n')
print('Measurements\n')
print(df, end = '\n\n')
print('Graphs')

# Creating the Visuals
plt.plot(dt['Girth'])
plt.title('Girth')
plt.ylabel('Metre')
plt.show()

plt.plot(dt['Height'])
plt.title('Height')
plt.ylabel('Metre')
plt.show()

plt.plot(dt['Volume'])
plt.title('Volume')
plt.ylabel('Cubic Metre')
plt.show()
```

Output

Tree measurements data

	Girth	Height	Volume
1	0.2	21.3	0.3
2	0.2	19.8	0.3
3	0.2	19.2	0.3
4	0.3	22.0	0.5
5	0.3	24.7	0.5
6	0.3	25.3	0.6
7	0.3	20.1	0.4
8	0.3	22.9	0.5
9	0.3	24.4	0.6
10	0.3	22.9	0.6
11	0.3	24.1	0.7
12	0.3	23.2	0.6
13	0.3	23.2	0.6
14	0.3	21.0	0.6
15	0.3	22.9	0.5

16	0.3	22.6	0.6
17	0.3	25.9	1.0
18	0.3	26.2	0.8
19	0.3	21.7	0.7
20	0.4	19.5	0.7
21	0.4	23.8	1.0
22	0.4	24.4	0.9
23	0.4	22.6	1.0
24	0.4	22.0	1.1
25	0.4	23.5	1.2
26	0.4	24.7	1.6
27	0.4	25.0	1.6
28	0.5	24.4	1.6
29	0.5	24.4	1.5
30	0.5	24.4	1.4
31	0.5	26.5	2.2

Note that in the `print` function we passed '\n\n' which means in the end parameter i.e. 2 lines of space as \n means a new line. If we haven't done that the
Tree measurements data
would be sticking with the data frame

123 PROJECT

Measurements

	Girth	Height	Volume
Maximum	0.52	26.54	2.18
Minimum	0.21	19.22	0.29
Average	0.34	23.18	0.85
Median	0.33	23.18	0.68
Mode	0.28	24.40	0.29

Graphs

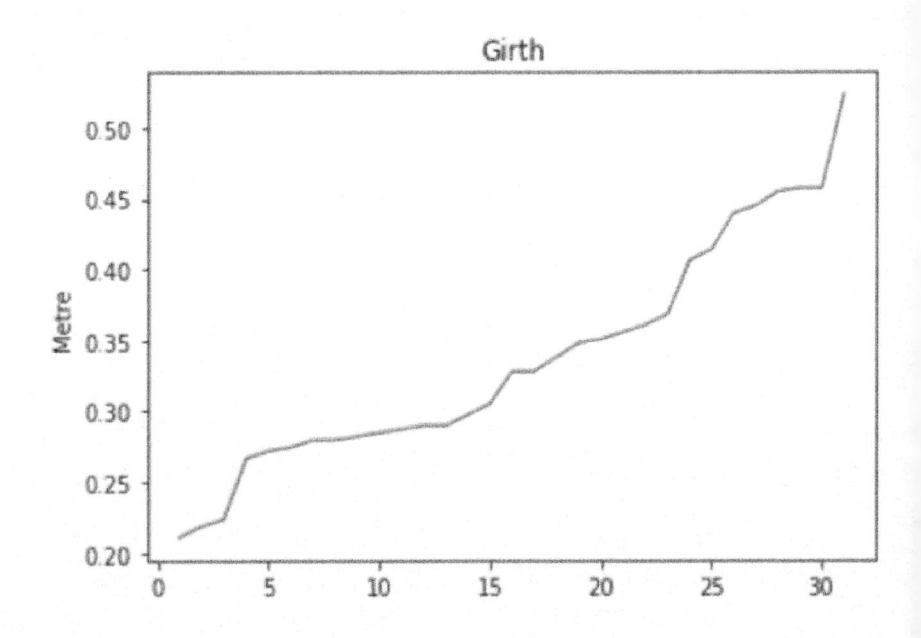

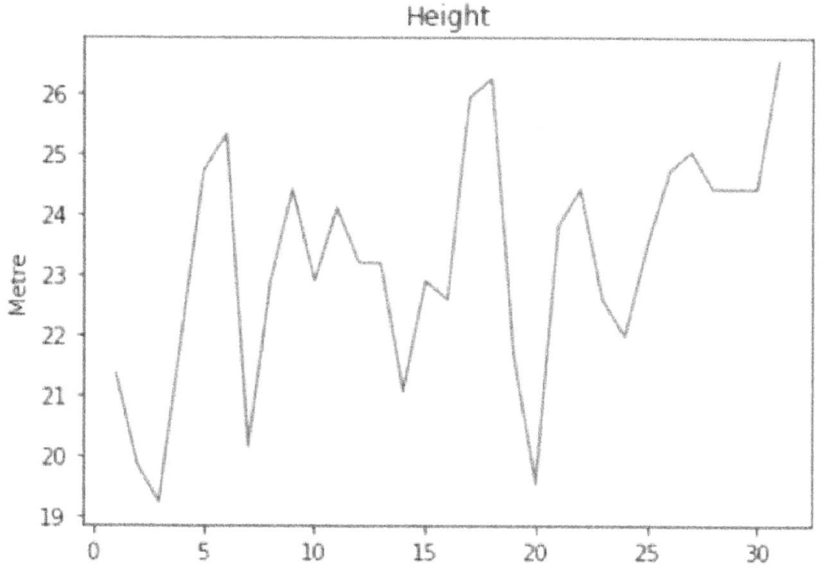
Height
Metre
26
25
24
23
22
21
20
19
0
5
10
15
20
25
30

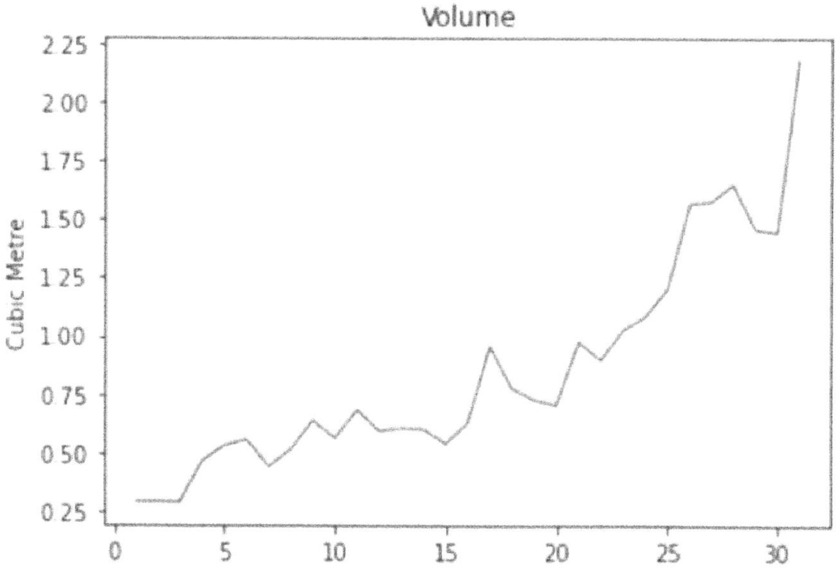
Volume
Cubic Metre
2.25
2.00
1.75
1.50
1.25
1.00
0.75
0.50
0.25
0
5
10
15
20
25
30

18 DATA SCIENCE

All the csv, txt, excel, etc. files used in this book can be find below:
http://bit.ly/dt_sc_sets

What now?

It been a while but you have completed this book, but that's not the end! You can check out the following books and choose them next:

Python for Complete Beginners

Learn programming from the basics with Python and become from a beginner to an advanced level programmer

Basic conncepts

All the basic programming concepts are covered in this book to help complete beginners

Machine Learning with Python

Beginners guide to machine learning

Models & Algorithms

Learn about different models and algorithms

You can find them through the below link:
http://bit.ly/PyBooks

I am not a regular at writing books so your thoughts about the book are precious. Please review the book and what do you think about the layout, presentation, explanation, etc. I'll be waiting to hear your thoughts:
http://bit.ly/DtSc_Rev

Printed in Great Britain
by Amazon